Lessons After The Bell

A man who views the world
the same at 50
as he did at 20
has wasted 30 years
of his life

—Muhammed Ali

BARNEY MARTLEW

WESTBOW®
PRESS
A DIVISION OF THOMAS NELSON
& ZONDERVAN

WestBow Press books may be ordered through booksellers or by contacting:

WestBow Press
A Division of Thomas Nelson & Zondervan
1663 Liberty Drive
Bloomington, IN 47403
www.westbowpress.com
1 (866) 928-1240

ISBN: 978-1-4908-7266-7 (sc)
ISBN: 978-1-4908-7265-0 (hc)
ISBN: 978-1-4908-7264-3 (e)

Library of Congress Control Number: 2015903804

Print information available on the last page.

WestBow Press rev. date: 04/24/2015

Contents

Acknowledgements

As you read the pages to follow you will learn, either by name or sometimes by reference to certain situations, many of the people to whom I am indebted. Some of them have taught me much, and others have proved themselves to be true friends. I value each of them and count myself fortunate to have association with people of such noble character.

There is also reference made to a few folks whom I'm not particularly fond of, but I am not fully dismissive of them either. Rather than hold a grudge or view someone with contempt I prefer to think of them with the levity of a song titled <u>That's Good, That's Bad</u> by Homer and Jethro (circa 1960, you can listen to it on YouTube). The gist of the song is that something we think of as being bad can lead to something good. As it applies to this book, the something bad is simply the lessons I learned the hard way, in which these folks had some involvement. But those lessons either caused me to change, or stopped me before something worse happened. In both types of situations something bad led to something good. So I am also indebted to this group, because something good came out of something bad. Besides, those guys are no longer in my life and I like it that way; another something good that came about by something bad.

There is a select group of folks I do want to acknowledge here. Their contributions to this book warrant these specific notes of appreciation.

Don Drumm, a friend whom I met while in Israel, provided expert editorial review and counsel on a large portion of this book. The quality of my writing improved with incorporation of each of his recommended changes.

Don is a gentle man, a gentleman, and a joy to be with. I appreciate his friendship and his concern for my well-being.

Honors need to be extended and my appreciation expressed, as well, to my friend George Stoms. His Dewey Decimal System[1] mind, willingness to proof the manuscript prior to publication, and encouragement that I allow neither complacency nor assumptions in my conveyance of thoughts added precision, clarity and continuity to my words.

My son and daughter both possess knowledge that exceeds mine in multiple areas. Their review of the book and counsel in their areas of expertise ensured both accuracy and an easy flow of information. I am proud of them, I love them, and I appreciate them.

There is a saying that goes: A prudent man surrounds himself with wise counsel.[2] I received that from Don, George, and my children.

Equally important, no, more important, is Pal, my wife. Life would be different without her. On a daily basis she demonstrates abiding love, through sickness and health, through richer and poorer, through good times and bad. Singer Tim McGraw has a song titled <u>Shotgun Rider</u> that does a pretty good job describing how I feel about her. (You can listen to that on YouTube, too.) All I would like to add to the lyrics is "What God has joined together..." He should get credit, too.

---

[1] The Dewey Decimal System is how libraries are organized in a complete and orderly fashion.

[2] Proverbs 1:5 from the Bible provides the foundation for this saying. Proverbs 13:20, and 15:22 may also be cited. Look them up. They are encouraging and worth reading.

So, Just What Was I Thinking?

I am not keen on laying my vulnerabilities out for the world to see, yet I am compelled to write about my experiences in the hope that others may benefit from them. Part of me can truthfully say I really don't care what people think about me, yet not all of me. No one wants to get blind-sided and have to endure the venomous assaults of contentious, condescending people. This is especially true when those doing the assault have a quickness of wit and eloquence of voice that exceed my capacity to respond and refute.

When I put things in their proper perspective though I realize I'd rather be me with all my foibles than others with their disingenuousness. I know I can be combative and respond to those with the condescending remarks in like manner, with all the mean words polite company is not supposed to use commingled with all the customary swear words in a plethora of combinations. I try to keep that part of me firmly under control though. The better response is to think of the contentious as being too insecure to face their failures and frustrations in life. Denial, after all, is not an uncommon protection mechanism, and proverbially, my skin is thicker than it used to be.

There are many aspects of the path I have walked in this life that I would not repeat if I had the option to do things over. Yet I am smart enough to know those aspects may be the biggest contributors to lessons learned. As the saying goes, bad decisions make good examples.

At this station in life I can say I am glad to still be part of the living, and believe the best is yet to come. This holds true for me personally and for many others. So I accept what has been and keep moving forward. With a hope that my experiences may benefit others I make myself vulnerable, and I write.

See if you can relate to any of this:

As I progressed through middle school, high school, and college, a sense of unsettledness walked with me. My concern was what I perceived to be a large disparity between what I hoped for and what I thought I might achieve. I knew how to dream big dreams, but lacked the confidence and understanding required to convert dreams into reality.

Insecurity causes one to think in silly ways and come to goofy conclusions. As a teenager I hoped for a prestigious career, yet fully expected I would become an assembly line worker at the local auto factory. The greatest reality, I deluded myself into thinking, was that if I went to college I might get to be a supervisor on the assembly line.

Though I yearned for an important title the real issue wasn't work or position. The real issue was controlling my unsettledness and living up to a perceived potential. I believed I possessed hidden talents, but I lacked confidence in my ability to draw them out.

So there is no misunderstanding, let me detour for a moment and say this: I don't disparage folks whose jobs involve assembly, manual labor, or skilled trades. I have worked the jobs of craftsmen and blue-collar America and have great respect for men and women in those positions. I have learned much from such individuals, and some of those lessons are included herein. With the maturity that comes with age I now think I would enjoy such a job along with the discipline, structure, predictability, and camaraderie that it offers.

As I look back and ponder my progression into adulthood I am aware that, at different periods in my life, significant people provided valuable input and expressed confidence to propel me forward. Their names don't mean anything to most people, but memories of them loom large in my mind. I include them here out of respect and appreciation for the gifts they gave me - their time, advice, and overall belief in my character. That last aspect, I now realize, reveals the high quality of each of these people's individual character. They were inclined to look past the facade I presented to the world around me.

A second reason for their inclusion is for the benefit of those who read this book; my mild attempt to change societal attitudes. I see value in proposing a different standard on which to gauge success, a different perspective; a innocuous manifestation of my contrarian nature.

We too often use money, power, and prestige as the metrics of choice to define success and accomplishment. In so doing we limit our parameters of evaluation, and perhaps, place emphasis on the wrong determinants of value. Why not use the edification of others as a basis of measurement for success, or the opportunity to encourage and provide direction to someone lost and wandering aimlessly? We pay lip service to the importance of positive, constructive interpersonal relationships, so why not use those as a better and more appropriate standard of measurement.

With emphasis on that last paragraph the people listed below are successful beyond belief. That, at least, is how they are viewed through my eyes.

* Dr. David E. Molyneaux, the senior pastor at First Presbyterian Church in Flint, Michigan, who befriended me in spite of my wild teenage ways;
* Don and Doris Orr, who did everything for me, short of (legally) adopting me as a second son;
* Vickie Bay's mom, who noted my abilities and got me pointed toward an engineering education;
* Heather MacKenzie's mom, who always had fresh baked cookies and a glass of milk to offer, and time to sit around the kitchen table and talk;
* Greg Whipple's parents, just plain good folks, who laughed with me and welcomed me into their home, even as they endured a family tragedy;
* And others whom you'll read about in the chapters ahead.

My wife of 36 years certainly belongs at the top of this list. For emphasis sake I have her at the bottom of the list. (You tend to remember that which you read last.) I'll leave that as a sufficient statement to convey her importance to me.

In snapshot form here is a chronology of my progression through life:

- As a teenager and young adult I made an unbelievable number of boneheaded mistakes. As a result there were many basic tenets of life and maturation that I missed.
- It took me until I turned 40 years of age to learn some of the things I should have realized at age 20.
- By age 50 I finally clued into some of the things I should have known by age 40. I concluded that learning should be caught up to age by the time I hit 60. I found that thought to be inspiring and encouraging.
- Giving reason for celebration, my age-50 conclusion came three years early. At age 57 I realized "I now get it; I now understand much of what I have missed through the years." My level of learning and comprehension was finally commensurate with my age and position in life. What a relief. A dogged effort to get caught up paid off.

What I have written so far is simply meant to set the foundation for the chapters that follow. This book wasn't conceived out of a desire to tell my life's story (it's actually kinda dull), but there are valuable life lessons I hope to pass on. Since most of those lessons come from my experiences I have to talk about me. My motivation is not self-adulation though. Rather, my compulsion to write is this: I prefer that no one make the mistakes I made, nor emulate my path through life. Some of my actions were made out of ignorance, others defiance; some were just poor judgment and planning. Much to my good fortune, and in spite of me behaving like me, I was also blessed along the way. I learned to mitigate the effects of things that held me back. So my first hope is that others won't make the same mistakes I made. My other hope is that those who read this book will forget my name, but benefit from my lessons learned.

The preceding paragraph conveys part of my motivation to write this book. The other part is a concern that there is a dearth of learning that comes from the experiences of others. That is bad. Experiential learning is an important component of the knowledge it takes to cultivate communities with meaning, purpose, and an opportunity to prosper. Experiential learning stands in opposition to lies being upheld as truths. In short, there is a big difference between theory and practice; between doing what is popular and doing what is right; between acting on public opinion, and acting on convictions; in using results and outcome as a basis for judgement rather than presenting intent as an poor excuse for foolish planning and decision making. Experiential learning enhances our understanding and appreciation of these differences. It enables us to recognize fallacies and make wise choices.

It is important to note that everything I have written is meant to end with a positive perspective. Presenting information with an inclination toward the negative, or with a suspicious or accusatory tone seems to be the norm of our society. Many prominent political figures are proficient at this and the media can't get enough of it. I prefer a different tact.

Stemming from a desire to be honest some of what I write may sound negative and somewhat condescending. That is not my purpose. My intent is to capture truth as truth. It also provides the opportunity to acknowledge that some things are a matter of perspective. Here is an example: As a pseudo-1960s radical (I was too young and uninformed to fully understand the crux of then-current issues); having spent 5 years teaching at a university; and with many years involvement with a lower-echelon segment of our society, I assumed that I was nonjudgmental. Yet one day I found myself thinking: "I don't get Goth, and why would anyone want tattoos, gages, or body piercings." At face value the desire for such stuff is beyond me and nothing I want to be a part of. That is a negative statement; it is also a true statement. As I pondered those thoughts further, though, others came to mind:

- I understand rebellion against perceived injustices and governmental structures that play errantly and liberally in their presentation of the truth. If that is the reason for any of the above, I get it; now I understand.

- I understand some things to be an expression of creativity. I get it.
- I understand some things are done out of a sense of belonging. I don't necessarily advocate that, but I get it.
- I am well aware that some people are motivated for reasons I may not understand and I am fine with that. Sometimes I get educated by such folks and gain insights I would otherwise not have. I benefit from differing opinions.
- I know that actions have consequences, and I am concerned that some may not appreciate the ramifications of that fact.
- I am equally aware that I cannot necessarily change the way others think. I do hope to educate and provide perspective, but the choice is always theirs.

So, its OK to speak the truth, even when it sounds negative. It may just be a matter of perspective, and it can lead to a beneficial outcome.

Enough of my ramblings. Let's turn the focus forward. To accomplish this we first need to establish a foundation upon which we can build.

A bit of introspection is a good thing. Regardless of your age, look back and consider your life thus far. What are the mountains you've had to climb, the obstacles to overcome? Who has stood beside you to help guide you? What have you learned in the process?

Take time to consider how your experiences and investment of time may benefit others. If no one guided and encouraged you as some did me, I am sorry. That has to be a hard realization. Use that, though, to help guide someone else. Be for someone what no one was for you. You'll be glad you did.

This book is meant to encourage anyone who needs encouraging. Part of human nature is to occasionally feel overwhelmed by present day struggles. With that comes self-doubt and a tendency to feel like the doors of opportunity are closed for the future. If this describes you, let me offer these words of encouragement: I understand... but don't allow your mind to park there for very long. Keep going. Don't stay stuck. You are not alone! Your life isn't over, and the best can be ahead.

Sometimes encouragement comes from someone shinning a light on a (better) path to give you guidance. Other times it comes by someone giving you a kick in the backside and telling you to "get going"! Occasionally I have needed both.

Through a particularly bleak period in my life I had to make a conscious and consistent effort to focus on examples of people who overcame adversity and had the *stick-to-it-ness* needed to succeed:

- Henry Ford had five business failures before he started his car company. That last venture worked out pretty well for him.
- Ray Kroc was 52 years old when he bought the franchise rights to a little restaurant owned by the McDonald brothers. That worked out pretty well for him.
- Harlan Sanders was a 6th grade dropout running a gas station/ diner before, at age 65, he started the restaurant chain we now know as KFC. That worked out pretty well for him, too.

The list goes on and on. So if you are struggling with your present circumstances here is some advice: Search for examples of folks who have overcome adversity; people who faced struggles similar to yours. This will help get your mind pointed in the right direction. Search the internet to facilitate the task, but qualify and confirm what you read because there is a lot of misinformation on the internet.

If you read the Bible take inspiration from a guy named Caleb, who said he was as strong and ready for battle at age 85 as he was at 40 (quite a claim; something to which I aspire); a guy who had to wait 45 years to get his compensation for being faithful and dutiful (something to which I do not aspire).[3]

---

[3] Reference Joshua 14: 6-13, found in the Old Testament section of the Bible

Get going.

For those who don't need encouraging, yet have this book in hand, you may still enjoy several of the chapters. You may find a perspective on matters that differs from yours. The book is meant to be simple, easy reading, and it may provoke thoughts and curiosities that you would not otherwise have considered.

One other thing I hope we accomplish is a systematic application of a process called *"pay it forward"*. The process is simple: Someone has done something for me and rather than seek payment or remuneration they ask only that I do something of equal or greater value for someone else. Thus, for whatever knowledge, insights, or benefits you glean from reading this book I ask that you pay it forward. Help someone else as they make their progression through life. You can make a positive difference in doing that.

There is often an after-the-fact benefit realized from *paying it forward*. Through the process you may grow weary, you may be vulnerable. But in the end you often discover that you got back more than you gave. That is cool!

The essays included herein are not deep thoughts, nor are they complex. They are meant to be lighthearted, positive, thought provoking, pleasing, and easy reading. Several essays may miss the lighthearted mark though. They are not yet written so I don't know exactly how they'll develop. The subject matter is dead-on serious and that may take precedence. I do, however, want them to be thought provoking and positive. I hope you enjoy them.

I wish you the best,
Barney Martlew
Kalamazoo, Michigan
October, 2013

Lessons After What Bell?

The various ways through which we learn are quite interesting when you stop and think about it. Sometimes the lessons are straightforward; sometimes they are learned through repeated exposure to a specific type of event. Some lessons are set to a specific block of time; permit me to use as reference the ring of a bell to denote the start, and another to denote the end. Other lessons fade in and out, with no well-defined start or stop. We learn through both methods.

Now consider this: The best way to learn a lesson or remember information is to put words to music. Think, for example, how many songs you know the lyrics to. Music affects all of us this way. We don't intentionally set out to memorize the words of a song, yet we learn them, and associate the words to different points in the music as the melody flows through our mind. Psychologists and other professionals who are knowledgeable in human behavior probably have a term for this and can explain the process whereby it happens. I don't know what that term is though. I just know it works.

Another way to remember information is by taking key points and associating them with a story. There is something about the human brain that processes information in such a manner. When association is made with something else our depth of understanding is enhanced. Equally important, our ability to recall the lesson also improves. Just as we connect words to music, we connect important points to associated stories.

On second thought I do know terms used to describe this process: cognitive thinking, and cognitive reasoning - a thought process whereby information is strung together in a reasonable, rational manner. When recalling one detail we also recall other details where an association has been made between them. Story telling creates those associations, the links between lessons and experiences.

A common practice used in storytelling to convey a point and create a sense of association is a metaphor. By definition, metaphors create the association between words and pictures that help us remember key points. For instance, when I looked up the word metaphor in my dictionary (The New Webster's Encyclopedic Dictionary of the English Language, copyright 1997) it referenced the title of a very old Christian hymn, "A Mighty Fortress is Our God", as an example.

So, what does God look like? I don't know. But when I think of a fortress, I think of strong, sturdy, long lasting, impenetrable, protective,... precisely the qualities and attributes we associate with God. I get it, metaphors work. By the way, I am a dinosaur, I like using the bound book dictionary I have rather than searching online. (Hey, another metaphor.)

As I write this sentence, a thought is on my mind, wondering if I'll get in trouble for citing copyrighted material? I don't know, but I guess I'll find out soon enough. Let's continue.

Now look at the jacket of this book. Both cover and title are meant to represent metaphors. I had three metaphors in mind when I started this project. Do you see them? Two should be clear and the third may be a bit obtuse. By some peoples way of thinking two of the concepts may be sufficiently similar that there is no significant difference. It's your call. I don't object to either interpretation. Here's how I look at it, though:

- The building represents an old time, one room schoolhouse. In days gone by children would walk from afar to attend school, and all ages would be together in the same room. A single teacher would provide the instruction for each subject and every level of learning. Unique to the one-room setting, the older children would help the younger ones with their studies. Once the bell rang, lessons began. Not only did the younger kids learn from the teacher, but from the older kids too. In effect the young ones learned from those who had previously been in their position. Also, the older ones enhanced their knowledge and understanding by repeating and explaining lessons to the younger ones. That created a sense of community between older and younger. *Lessons after the bell* were both formal instruction coming from the teacher, and the informal reinforcement by peers and older kids' involvements. In similar manner lessons of life come from both formal and informal sources.

• Or the building may represent an old country church. Not many examples exist of this today but there was a time where it was common for a community to be called together by the Sunday morning ringing of a church bell.

Prior to World War I, North America, both the United States and Canada, were primarily agrarian societies. Most people lived on farms or in rural settings. City populations were not nearly the size they are today.

Life in those days was physically hard - hard, hard, hard. Much of the work performed was by manual labor. Automation, to the extent it existed, was very basic. Talk to a farmer about an eight hour work day and he'd tell you he had two of those six days a week; talk about a 40 hour work week, and he'd tell you his 40 hours started about an hour before sun up on Monday, and ended around noon on Wednesday. He'd then go on to say he still had 3 1/2 days to go before he got a day of rest. And there were still chores to do, even on that day.

Life was emotionally hard, too. Farming accidents were prevalent, and that brought hardship to many. Infant mortality was off the charts, as were the number of women who died during childbirth, once the leading cause of death for the female gender. Life expectancy was significantly less than today. By the time you hit age 60 your body was simply worn out.

City life was equally challenging, with all the hardships of farm life and more. Fraternal organizations such as the Benevolent Protective Order of the Elks (BPOE, known today as the Elks Club), the Moose Club, and other social groups formed for two reasons. One was they provided the core for the social structure of subgroups in a community - the chance for men to gather and families to gather with others. The other reason, of particular importance to a family-focused working man, was that these groups provided a safety net in times of serious injury or a premature death. Every member of such organization knew that if he died and left a family behind there was a group of others who would care for them.

By today's standards both rural life and city life were hard, but a respite came with Sundays. The morning tolling of the church bell served as an early model of a public address system. It notified folks that the time had come to set aside work obligations for a while and change the focus of their efforts. Even those who weren't spiritually minded benefitted. The majority of the population established the practices and mores of society that enabled communities to function and prosper.

Following Sunday morning church there was a relative day of rest; a chance to interact with others. The morning was for spiritual worship and education; the afternoon allowed the opportunity for relaxation and fellowship with others. Both morning and afternoon provided opportunities for learning - lessons after the (church) bell.

Toil and hardship compel folks to set priorities and decide what the fundamental needs and purpose of life are. These Sunday opportunities were embraced by most of the population. Mundane incidentals were set aside for more important aspects of life and living.

- Now think about a boxer, metaphor number three. The lessons here may be a bit less obvious, but they are still very real. Where a boxer's education begins and where it ends are two completely different environments. Two boxers enter a ring ready for a match - healthy, prepared, confident. Each has subjected himself to intense physical training and has come to the match mentally prepared; each has aspirations of winning. Both have subjected themselves to disciplined regimens, and sought to learn about their opponent's fighting style. Regarding the upcoming match both boxers have a theoretical knowledge of what may happen, formal education. The real education comes after the bell rings and the fight starts - lessons after the bell - a significant difference between preparation and application; what works in theory, and what works in practice. One will prevail, both will be bruised and bloodied; both learn.

Boxers learn about being in the ring by being in the ring. It is there where they hone the disciplines of their sport, compete, and sometimes fail. A wise boxer analyzes his failures to assess what went wrong, modifies his style, perfects his skills, and moves on, improved, to compete again. A lost match (failure) typically doesn't thwart a boxer from continuing in his profession, and he doesn't dwell on things that went wrong. But he does learn from them.

These metaphors represent how we go through life and how we learn. A large portion of the process comes about in clean, orderly environments. Home instruction, schools, colleges, churches and synagogues provide structure, answer questions, and educate. These, along with other similar affiliations, accomplish the formal aspects of education and development, and provide the foundation of learning. The informal components - experiencing hardships; learning through personal attempts at accomplishments, both successes and failures; and learning through the experiences of others - are equally important. The former provides a framework for learning; the latter builds on that framework through experience. When coupled together they enhance comprehension, understanding, and wisdom.

To sum this up let's go back to the analogy of the boxer for a moment:

- As the boxer prepares for his fight he gains knowledge. His preparation is his formal education. The converse is also true: his formal education is his preparation. Both mental and physical efforts are required.
- Regardless of whether he wins or loses, as the boxer endures the pummeling of the match he gains experience which enhances his comprehension of what it takes to prevail. The environment of the boxing ring is where the informal education occurs, and it creates a level of knowledge called wisdom.

Wisdom is the goal. Wisdom is the light that illuminates the path ahead. It is the foundation that supports sound decisions. Seek wisdom. It comes from experiential learning, both yours and that which you glean from others.

Thank You Ms. Johnson, Wherever You Are

Thank you Ms. Johnson. You inspired me to want to learn. For the better, you were an amazing influence in my life.

Eleventh grade was an epochal year for me, at least in terms of understanding math, and the decision I made to apply myself. Up to that point anything associated with school and learning caused a mental malfunction. It wasn't a case of not comprehending whatever the subject of the hour was, I just didn't care. I'd sit in class out of obligation and watch the minutes of the hour go by: a circular analog clock with three hands - a red one that swept the circle once every 60 seconds; a long black hand that took 60 times as long to complete the same task; and a short black hand that moved 30 degrees around a circle in the same amount of time it took the other black hand to go a full 360 degrees. One hour, then on to the next class and the next clock to watch.

Being the annoying adolescent I was definitely irritated the situation. In fact it was a root cause of the problem. Though not my intention, I made myself unlikeable. I managed to frustrate one middle school math teacher to the point where she screamed at me. To this day I remember her words: "Don't ever become an architect or engineer! You're terrible at math!" My initial reaction was to think: "How do I know what I want to be, I'm only 13 years old." But I believed her. A scowling, semi-maniacal authority figure told me something and I figured that since she said it, it must be true.

The next couple years became a self-fulfilling prophecy reinforced by subsequent teachers. My memory is that they wrote me off prematurely.

Looking back, they would probably tell you I was an annoying, impetuous kid who made their job difficult.

By the time I hit eleventh grade I was rebellious, arrogant, and cocky. I was also very insecure so I had to put on a boastful front - a survival mode instinct.

Enter Ms. Johnson, my 11th grade math teacher. She chose to treat me different than others had. Rather than write me off, she saw through my facade. I remember her words too (kinda): "You can be good at math if you apply yourself." She didn't tell me I was smart (how would she know), rather her encouragement came as a challenge: "Work hard. It doesn't come easy, but you'll figure it out."

Given my teenage inclination toward self-absorption I still marvel that a person who should have had no influence in my life became a source of inspiration. What I find interesting is that, as a result of her expressed confidence in me, not only did my math skills improve but my performance in every other class improved as well. Out of concern that Ms. Johnson might talk with my other teachers (further evidence of teenage self-absorption) I didn't want to disappoint her or give her reason to lose confidence in me.

A foundational truth came into play through those events: When someone expresses confidence in you in one area, you naturally want to improve in other areas too.

So in the spirit of Ms. Johnson let me express confidence in you. It is legitimate for me to do that because most people simply get overwhelmed at times and don't know what the right thing to do is. It has nothing to do with intellectual capability. Rather, it pertains to being organized, setting goals, and moving forward.

Ms. Johnson had a series of rules she used to get us through the anxieties of learning math. Those rules have application to life and living as well:

- **Math takes time. You can't just read the pages of a book and plough through math. It takes time to work through the process.** The words *math* and *life* can be used interchangeably and the rule will still apply. Life takes time, and you have to work through the process. The goal isn't to avoid conflicts nor avoid making mistakes; the goal should be to learn and move forward. All of us experience successes and failures, so use both to your benefit. Learn, improve, and move forward.

- **Think of what you know, and what is being asked.**
  This rule applies to deciding which equation should be used to solve a problem. By looking at the information provided you can discard all the math equations that don't fit. For example, if the information provided deals with radians, degrees, and angles, you know you have either a geometry or trigonometry problem to solve. Thus you don't need to consider math equations that deal with finance or algebra because those equations can't use the information provided. Focus and simplify.

Focus and simplify is an important discipline to develop in life as well. There is a lot of "noise" (distractions, promises, wants, and the opinion of others) that clamor for our attention. Politicians use this to their advantage, as do advertisers. Both manipulate human emotions to achieve their own goals. Our challenge is to separate out all the noise, and make decisions based on sound reasoning and factors we know to be true.

- **Break big problems down into their individual components. Treat each big problem as a cluster of little problems. They are easier to understand that way. Then solve the individual little problems.**
  This needs no explanation as the principle applies in life just as it does in mathematics. There is a caveat to this that is worth mentioning though. Complex problems often seem that way because we let noise - the details that scream the loudest - distract us. That is just part of human nature. As we learn to dissociate

ourselves with the urgency of the moment we also develop the skill to break a complex issue into root causes and secondary issues. Root causes, also referred to as *primary issues*, are those that control the overall outcome. Secondary issues can be thought of as minor details. They may be important but they are not at the heart of the matter. Secondary issues are conditional on, and are subject to, primary issues.

Standard operating procedure in dealing with complex issues is to break the problem down into primary and secondary components. Then work on solving the primary issues. In doing so many of the secondary issues typically go away, or become sufficiently insignificant that they can be easily resolved later.

You have the opportunity to influence other people just as Ms. Johnson influenced me. It is not necessary that you be a teacher, nor even a person of authority. Coworkers, friends, relatives, neighbors, and others may be influenced by what they see you do, and hear what you say. Socio-economic factors do not necessarily limit the extent of your influence either. You may be beaten down, broke, and unable to speak in full sentences, but you may also know something that someone of a different stature needs to know. The impact you have on others can be either for better or for worse; positive or negative. You get to decide which it will be.

Corrie ten Boom

YAD VASHEM IS A MUST-SEE DESTINATION ON YOUR NEXT TRIP TO ISRAEL!

Never have I seen such a statement in a travel brochure. I doubt I ever will.

Yad Vashem is a memorial and museum located in Jerusalem, Israel. It was established in 1953 by the Israeli government eight years after the end of World War II and five years after formation of the modern-day nation of Israel. Its purpose is to honor Jewish victims of the Holocaust, both those who lost their lives and those who survived. Though the buildings and exhibits are complete, the museum and memorial are a work in process. For any Holocaust survivors who may still be alive and are correspondingly willing to do so, the Yad Vashem Foundation records their stories for inclusion as part of an everlasting archive. The stories are also added to an audio track of others' stories and played in continuum in a listening area. The purpose is that these people be given a platform on which they may share their experiences so that we, being thus educated, may never forget.

One can walk the length of an upward sloping center concourse and be through the main building in a matter of minutes. A full glass wall at the exit end - what architects refer to as a curtain wall - allows ample light from outside for you to find your way.

An alternative is to spend a full day walking through the exhibits, and in effect, take a walk through history. Rooms are positioned on the left and right sides; you traverse back and forth across the concourse as you view exhibits, read information plaques, observe video clips, and listen to audio recordings. This configuration, along with a change in lighting intensity - dimmer in the exhibit rooms, brighter in the center concourse - are meant to symbolize two things:

1. Traversing is meant to replicate the progression of history. History does not unfold in a predictable straight line, nor should its presentation.
2. The difference in lighting plays on one of the tenets of Judaism. No matter how dark the present, there is always hope for the future. The muted lighting of the exhibit rooms represent the present; the bright illumination of the center concourse represents hope. The upward slope of the concourse likewise plays into symbolism - remain faithful and progress upward (spiritually) toward God.

People's emotions differ as they tour Yad Vashem. I doubt you will find anyone festive and outwardly joyous while there, but it's not necessarily a sorrowful place either. It's not meant to be. The memorial that sits atop the U.S.S. Arizona in Pearl Harbor, Hawaii is solemn; Yad Vashem seems different. Yad Vashem is certainly sobering and informative. Educated, aware, and hopeful may be the mood the designers want visitors to take with them.

The path that runs between the parking area and the main exhibit building is known as The Avenue of the Righteous Among the Nations. This area and an adjacent garden were developed to honor non-Jews who risked great personal suffering by aiding Jews as they attempted to hide or flee from their persecutors. A woman from the Netherlands by the name of Corrie ten Boom was so honored on December 12, 1967. A tree was planted on The Avenue in recognition of her devotion, service and sacrifice.

Corrie ten Boom (1892 - 1983) and her sister Betsie lived with their father Casper in Haarlem, Holland during the Nazi occupation of World War II. They, along with other family members, hid Jews and clandestinely worked with the Dutch underground to provide safe passage for those fleeing certain death. On February 28, 1944 they were caught, arrested, and imprisoned. Casper, an old man at this point, died ten days following his arrest; Betsie and Corrie ended up at the Ravensbruck death camp in Germany. Betsie died in Ravensbruck in December of that same year. Of the three, only Corrie survived.

Corrie was released prior to the war's end. She noted that it came about as a result of a clerical error, and it occurred one week before all women at the camp of her age were put to death. (For the full story read Corrie's autobiography The Hiding Place. It is a book worth reading.)

Following her release Corrie managed to return to the Netherlands. At war's end she began attending to the emotional devastations that remained. In particular, she worked to heal the emotional scars carried by those who had collaborated with the Nazi - once powerful, they were now ostracized and abused. Corrie's care and concern for others took her back to Germany. There she tells the story of meeting and forgiving a man she recognized who had been a particularly vicious guard at Ravensbruck.

Corrie's hallmark was her ability to forgive. She attributed that to her devotion to Jesus Christ and her firm belief in the goodness and graciousness of God. Corrie likened forgiveness to letting go of the rope attached to a bell: As long as you hold onto the rope, the bell keeps ringing; the ringing doesn't stop until you let go. Having seen the devastation of so many, she also wisely noted that it is those who are able to forgive that are best able to rebuild their lives.

In later years Corrie traveled the world as a counselor and motivational speaker. She helped many work through spiritual and emotional devastation, and she died peacefully at an old age.

A willingness to forgive is a lesson that took me a long time to learn. My approach to handling conflict and contending with the wounds of wrongs received was to hold in my emotions, say nothing, and be stoic. That was not a good approach. It accomplished nothing and it precluded me from dealing with the issues. Worse, by not dealing with an issue even perceived slights grew in size, and anger boiled within. When the anger eventually exploded out of me there was a lot of carnage left in the aftermath. Nothing was resolved and there was now even more damage to contend with.

I don't recall what it was that brought about a change where I learned to forgive and let go. It was a work in process and it didn't come all at once. Over time it does become more of a natural response, but certainly not initially.

In certain situations it may be prudent to force yourself to <u>not</u> think about something or someone for a set span of time. Allow anger, maybe rage, time to abate. Purposefully put distance between yourself and someone else. This is one step in the process. It is not avoidance, it is simply controlling a situation that needs firm controls applied to it. Its constructive purpose is to allow time for emotional preparation prior to confronting a difficult task.

Under the constraint of the paragraph above, I realized that the best way to deal with bad situations and contentious people is <u>to</u> deal with them. This is very important. Acquiescence, avoidance, and holding anger in accomplishes nothing. It is important to keep emotions at bay. Let facts, logic, wise decisions and calm confrontation drive your actions. Then let go.

Maybe this is one of those rare occasions where it's OK to say "It's all about me": It's about me and how I handle a situation, not another person and how they handle it. When you forgive it puts you in a better position to move on and rebuild.

It helps to think of Corrie, too. No matter how I have been wronged, I have not suffered nearly as much as she and others have.

Forgiving others is a gift you give yourself. When you forgive you make a conscious, intelligent decision to not waste your time, energy, and peace of mind hating another person.

Priorities, and a Guy Named Bonhoeffer

The priorities you set in life will dictate your actions. They compel you to conform to mores and social standards, or set you apart and embolden you to strive for something else. They may lead you to do what is right more so than what is popular.

By your priorities you may be a catalyst for change and thus influence an entire culture's way of thinking. Conversely, they may make you a recipient for others' disassociation, refutes, and scorn; a lightning rod for verbal abuse and contempt; or even a recipient of physical harm. Priorities set for the common good may benefit others long after your sphere of influence has passed. Misplaced priorities may bring burden and hardship for you and those close to you. Likewise, misplaced priorities sometimes have long-term lingering effects.

Priorities work for you or against you, and to others it may not be clearly discernible which is which. The metrics you use for evaluation may be different than the units of measurement more commonly used. That, too, comes about simply by the priorities you set.

In practical application priorities may be well founded or misplaced. They may benefit you at the expense of others; benefit you with no effect on others; or benefit you and others. They may work against you and be your sole burden to bear, or they may drag others down with you. On that thought it is appropriate to offer an admonition to choose your priorities well.

When someone says "I don't care what others think about me" there are different ways to interpret that statement. Two extremes of interpretation may be: "I care, but what I have set as a priority takes precedence, so that has to drive my actions"; to "What others think of me is so low on my priority list that it doesn't really matter." Priorities thus become a weighted variable.

Priorities are priorities, but they are not absolutes. They can be compromised or sometimes completely disregarded. So in that regard it may be appropriate to say keeping your priorities has to be a priority in itself.

External factors may at times inhibit the implementation of your priorities. Even in these times though, priorities still act as our guiding principles. Like a bungee cord when stretched, they act as a tether. When the stretching is relaxed they bring us back to a fixed point.

A couple more analogies apply here:
- Priorities may act like an anchor to hold us fast, and secure us against the storms of life.
- Priorities may act like a guiding star as we are prone to wonder, or as we get knocked about by daily pressures. In the long run they set the path we follow.

Well-founded priorities are a good thing. Choose them well.

Integrity as a priority was apparently pretty high on the list for a guy named Dietrich Bonhoeffer. It cost him his life.

Dietrich Bonhoeffer was born into a well-educated German family in 1906. His dad was a professor of psychiatry at the University of Berlin and his mom was college degreed, a rarity for women at that time. The family came from an affluent, aristocratic background, though the parents encouraged their children in liberal pursuits. The children (8 total) were intellectually gifted, and Dietrich had the added achievement of great musical accomplishment in that he played the piano well. The parents, and subsequently the children, were not necessarily unreligious people, but spiritual matters held only a modest place of concern to them through Dietrich's formative years. At age 14 Dietrich shocked his family with his announcement that he planned to pursue a career in theology (the study of divine things and religious truths) and Christian ministry. This evoked a certain amount of protest, opposition, and ridicule from some family members, but Dietrich's priorities were set.

At age 24 Bonhoeffer received a fellowship to attend Union Theological Seminary in New York City. 1930 and 1931 thus found him living in America. While in New York Bonhoeffer grew dissatisfied with the churches he attended, finding them to be places where people showed up on Sunday mornings, but not necessarily God. He thus started attending a black congregational church in the Harlem section of New York City with fellow seminarian Frank Fisher, a black student from Alabama. There Bonhoeffer found the spiritual vitality and fellowship he sought, with worship enhanced by the music of the church. As an accomplished musician that solidified his connection to the congregation. Many believe that Bonhoeffer's observations of how blacks were treated in America strongly influenced his future reactions to the waves of contempt and hatred that were building in Germany against the Jews.

Bonhoeffer's return to Germany occurred at the same time as the rise of Nazism, and an inevitable clash of priorities was soon to ensue:

- Adolf Hitler was elected chancellor of Germany, and systematic suppression of the Jews commenced.
- Bonhoeffer published an essay titled <u>The Church and the Jewish Question</u>, which called into question how the organized church would respond to abuses perpetrated by Nazis against Jews.

- Many German churches supported Hitler, with some even referring to him as the messiah. (Nationalism got in the way of spiritual priorities, which is a pretty good indication of those churches' level of spiritual vitality. Sadly today, many churches do something similar. They have confused humanism and social do-good-ism with seeking to honor God and living according to his word.)
- Bonhoeffer and others organized the *Confessing Church*, which stood against the established religious structure of Germany under the Nazi regime.

- The Nazis banned Bonhoeffer from speaking or teaching publicly.
- Bonhoeffer taught at an "underground" seminary.

- Over time the *Confessing Church,* under intense pressure, became less and less inclined to speak out against Hitler.
- Bonhoeffer moved from a pacifist position to an activist role, clandestinely acting to help Jews escape persecution.

In June, 1939 Bonhoeffer sailed back to America having accepted a university position as a guest lecturer. He could have stayed and been freed from the increasing repression he personally experienced in Germany. Within a month of his arrival, however, he returned to Germany, writing to a friend: "I have made a mistake in coming to America. I must live through this difficult period in our national history with the Christian people of Germany. I will have no right to participate in the reconstruction of Christian life in Germany after the war if I do not share the trials of this time with my people."[4]

Bonhoeffer's activism expanded from helping Jews escape to being part of a plot to overthrow the Third Reich. He also participated in a plot to assassinate Hitler, the depth of his involvement, though, I am not knowledgeable enough to comment on.

In April, 1943 Bonhoeffer's clandestine activities were discovered. He was arrested and imprisoned. In April, 1945, under a direct order from Hitler, he was hanged at the Flossenburg extermination camp. Bonhoeffer was 39 years old. His death occurred less than a month before Hitler's suicide and the collapse of Nazi Germany.

Years later a doctor who had witnessed Bonhoeffer's execution wrote: "I saw Pastor Bonhoeffer... kneeling on the floor praying fervently to his God. I was most deeply moved by the way this lovable man prayed, so devout and so certain that God heard his prayer. At the place of execution he again said a prayer and then climbed the steps to the gallows, brave and

---

[4] Dietrich Bonhoeffer: A Biography, Eberhard Bethge

composed. His death ensued in a few seconds. In the almost 50 years that I have worked as a doctor, I have hardly ever seen a man die so entirely submissive to the will of God."[5]

Could I do the same?

I found a quote that is worth thinking about:

> "Who stands firm? Only the one for whom the final standard is not his reason, his principles, his conscience, his freedom, his virtue, but who is ready to sacrifice all these, when in faith and sole allegiance to God he is called to obedient and responsible action: the responsible person, whose life will be nothing but an answer to God's question and call." - Dietrich Bonhoeffer[6]

The priorities you set in life will dictate your actions. They will either compel you to conform to mores and social standards, or set you apart and embolden you to strive for something different. As with Bonhoeffer, they may lead you to do what is right more so than what is popular.

Priorities work for you or against you, and to an outsider it may not be clearly discernible which is which. The metrics you use for evaluation may be different than the units of measurement more commonly used by others. Others may, at a later time, come to realize what you already know to be true.

---

[5] Ibid
[6] Letter and Papers from Prison, D.B.

Evidence Documented in History

Let's start with things we can agree on. Maybe we'll have other points to argue about later.

Here are some historic facts regarding ancient conquests in the Middle East:

- Babylon, under the leadership of King Nebuchadnezzar, conquered the land of Judah in 586 BC. Battles between the two nations had been on-again/off-again for more than twenty years. During that time there were three occurrences where captives from Judah were taken to Babylon. The land of Judah is now known as the current-day country of Israel which includes, specifically, the city of Jerusalem. Ancient-day Babylon is modern-day Iraq.
- Persia, under the reign of King Cyrus, conquered Babylon in the year 539 BC. He took possession of everything Babylon had conquered. Ancient-day Persia is current-day Iran.
- Persia was conquered by Alexander the Great of Greece in the year 330 BC.
- Rome conquered Greece in 146 BC. Control of all the above passed on, as would be expected. All the land previously known as Judah was generically referred to as Judea.
- Judea, and Jerusalem specifically, were still under the control of Rome at the time of Jesus' birth. Caesar Augustus was the ruler of Rome at that time. Many years earlier he appointed a guy named Herod (known through antiquity as Herod the Great) to be in charge of Judea. Herod seized this opportunity to appoint himself king of the Jews, the primary occupants of Judea. By the time of Jesus' birth Herod was in the final years of his life.

- Herod was ultra wealthy and a phenomenal builder, but he was not a very nice guy. He was paranoid, and he made many enemies. Making enemies tends to happen when you indiscriminately kill people, and Herod did a lot of people-killing. He also died a not-very-nice death. During his reign he built (well actually, ordered to be built, he didn't do any of the physical labor himself) the Mediterranean port city of Caesarea Maritima, a desert palace called Masada, and the Temple Mount in Jerusalem where the Muslim shrine the Dome of the Rock is now located. Archeologists, to this day, are still amazed by what Herod built.

Well, that pretty much sums things up. Let us go back to the beginning and fill in a few details about one of the captives taken to Babylon.

A young guy named Daniel became part of King Nebuchadnezzer's booty when Babylon thumped the king of Judah. Historians speculate Daniel was 16-18 years old at the time. He was probably part of the first group of exiles to be taken to Babylon, which occurred in 605 BC. Daniel's story is told in the first six chapters of the Book of Daniel, found in the Old Testament of the Bible. The conquests of Babylon and Persia are also documented in archeological artifacts known as the Babylonian Tablets.

Historic records reveal that standard operating procedures of this era, when one nation conquered another, was for a portion of the loser's population to be killed. Another portion would be sent into exile, the idea being that they should intermingle with and marry people of their new nation, and thus lose their former national identity. Some people were sold into slavery, and a portion of the original population was allowed to remain. It was usually the poor, aged, and infirm who were left behind, those who were of no value to the conquerors. New inhabitants would be brought in to the conquered land to intermingle with those who remained, another action meant to homogenize national identity.

Daniel was selected to be part of a privileged group of exiles, sort of. Being young, smart, and handsome, he became a member of a group that was to be educated in Babylonian ways, history, and culture, with the intent being

21

to serve Babylon's king in a governmental capacity. All of that is good. By the standards of those days it meant he would live a reasonably good life. There is always a catch, though; in the case of Daniel, probably two:

- Daniel was a devout Jew, and his home was Jerusalem. Being sent to Babylon would take him from family and the land that he loved, the place of his birth. Also, the education he was to receive was meant to strip away his old allegiances, a faith and a devotion to God that he did not want to let go of.
- The Biblical account says the king "instructed Ashpenaz, the master of his eunuchs" to select the group of which Daniel would become a part.[7] Some historians interpret this phrase to mean Dan underwent a surgical procedure to become part of that which Ashpenaz was master of. Who knows what happened, but there is high probability in favor of something I prefer to not think about. Regardless, the story doesn't end there.

People who hold fast to their Jewish faith follow a strict diet, a rule of order for eating, with many mandates regarding what is allowed and what is not. This is true even to this day. You will not, for example, hear a devout Jew order a bacon cheeseburger at a restaurant. That would violate two prohibitions: one against eating pork; the other against eating dairy and meat at the same meal.

Maintaining a strict diet, one that did not violate his beliefs, was Daniel's first challenge. He devised a strategy and stuck to it. I don't think the guy was rebellious, he was probably quite compliant on issues that didn't matter, but he knew his limitations on issues that did. He studied and learned, and according to the historic record, excelled in knowledge and learning.

Daniel pulled off quite a feat. He didn't shortchange his beliefs, yet he committed himself to performing well in a situation that obligated him to do so. The result was that he earned the trust of King Nebuchadnezzer.

---

[7] Reference Daniel 1: 3-4

Daniel was put in an authority and leadership position in the king's administration.

Working for people who have an over-inflated opinion of themselves and their accomplishments can be challenging, and Daniel certainly encountered that with Nebuchadnezzer. Through these ordeals Daniel maintained his composure and kept doing what he believed to be the right thing to do. As a devout Jew, a faith he never let go of, he spent much time praying and seeking God's guidance through difficult situations. The priorities by which Daniel chose to live his life served him well. It is worth noting that the indoctrinations Daniel received regarding Babylonian culture and history had no effect on his faith or priorities. Daniel didn't let his career advancements alter his principles either. He performed his tasks well, but shunned personal praise and glory.

Just as with modern-day leaders, kings came and kings went. Nebuchadnezzer eventually grew old and died, but Daniel continued in service to his successors. The Kingship eventually landed on a guy named Nabonidus, and as it pertains to Daniel, nothing was said about him. The historic records are not fully clear, yet it is readily accepted that Nabonidus spent a lot of time away from Babylon. When he was off on journeys establishing trade routes, fighting battles, or enjoying other vistas, his son Belshazzar was left in charge of the country as co-regent. Belshazzar was thus referred to as king.

It appears that Belshazzar was something of a party animal who was more interested in the affairs of Belshazzar than he was the affairs of the kingdom. On a night of heavy drinking and revery Babylon was conquered by an opposing military force. One interpretation of the archeological record is that the Medo-Persian army diverted the waters of the Euphrates River which flowed through the capitol city. The water gate that would block access through the river portal was left unsecured. Guards who were supposed to protect the city may have been goof offs, or they may have been bribed. In any event the Medo-Persians marched into the city on a dry river bed. Belshazzar was slain, but many historians believe widespread slaughter did not occur. The government structure was left largely intact. Darius the Mede took over Babylon on behalf of Cyrus, King of Persia.

Daniel served his new employer with the same devotion to duty with which he had served others. In so doing he earned the trust of Darius. Daniel became the highest government official in Darius' administration and continued to do his tasks well.

In what we would now call his post-retirement years Daniel was allowed to return to Jerusalem, the place of his birth. After more than sixty years of responsibly serving others, Daniel returned home.

If you read the Biblical account of Daniel there are a number of lessons and observations to be gleaned:

- Of the original group of captives when Nebuchadnezzer first came on the scene, Daniel had three friends. As a group of four they provided each other with high levels of support and accountability. It is important to have friends like that, folks who will buoy your spirits during fatiguing, frustrating times; folks who will make themselves vulnerable to hold you accountable to do the right thing when you are inclined to do something else. Those are the type of people who will stand by you both in good times and in bad, knowing that you will also do the same for them.

- Daniel committed himself to making the best of bad situations, regardless of how bad the situations got. He kept his faith and trust in God and let everything else give way to his beliefs. Another way to say this is if God is in control, and God has your best interests in mind, then even bad situations must have a reason for good behind them. They do not happen by circumstance. This is a good point to remember when it seems like life is moving against you.

- Daniel was neither interested in being part of the in-crowd, high society, or whatever you want to term it, nor was he willing to compromise his core principles to conform to others. Those who matter repeatedly took notice of this, and Daniel's wealth and influence grew even though they were not his pursuits.

- When the opportunities for self-adulation came, Daniel instead turned the praise and recognition toward God. No one could ever accuse Daniel of having a self-inflicted terminally bruised back. (He didn't pat himself on the back.)

- Free from ulterior motives or hidden agendas, Daniel simply committed himself to being responsible and dutiful and doing his assigned tasks well. Daniel advanced and prospered above others, and he did it without stepping on other people through the process.

Those are all good lessons to observe and understand.

So where is the conflict that gives us something to argue about? That comes only with those who would say this may be a nice story, but it is just a made-up story because the Bible is just made up and is not factual. There are many who tow that line, and that notion is widely accepted.

If you fall into that camp I encourage you to look at the plethora of evidence in the historical, geographical, geological, and archeological records, all of which verify the accuracy and validity of what is written. You may not be able to satisfy every question that will arise, but impressed by the evidence, you may start to see things in a way you have not previously considered.

In a sense it is almost comical. People read something in the Bible that doesn't fit with other things they have heard, or things they want to believe, so they assume the Bible is wrong. That happened with the story of Belshazzar:

> There was a time when the archeological record supported the belief that Nabonidus was (the sole) king of Babylon at the time of its fall. People therefore assumed the Bible was wrong because of its statements regarding Belshazzar. That line of reason held until further archeological evidence provided documentation showing Nabonidus spent much of his time away from the kingdom, and left his son in charge. It then became clear that what the Bible states provided more accurate, detailed information than what was commonly believed to be true.

In similar fashion, evidence regarding Pontius Pilate, the guy in charge of Jerusalem at the time of Jesus' death:

> There was a time when archeologists questioned the existence of such a person because the only known reference to him was found in the Bible. You can't fault them for being doubtful. By the nature of their profession they try to uncover the evidence of truth by sorting through tidbits of antiquity. In 1961 though, a block of limestone bearing the name of Pontius Pilate was found in Caesarea Maritima, a town located about 60 miles from Jerusalem (a two day journey at the time of Pilate). This new discovery surfaced evidence that challenged and invalidated the then-currently-held beliefs.

So maybe instead of doubting a source that has yet to be proven false we should instead look kindly on the archeologists and give them a chance to catch up to the truth. They have a lot of artifacts to examine, and a lot of history to dig through.

Let me conclude with this comment: You cheat yourself if you attempt to pick and choose your way through the Bible. By choosing *"some of this"* to believe in, but rejecting *"some of that other stuff"* you simply reduce God down to your level of comprehension. In doing so you limit his influence in your life and his opportunity to educate you. You do not need to apologize for God. His level of knowledge is undoubtably greater and more vast than ours. He knows the beginning and the end of everything, cause and effect, every nuance, and every reason. You may not like some things the Bible says, but there is nothing therein that can be or has been proved false.

Vancouver in September

Our flight originated somewhere in Michigan. I don't recall whether we left from Kalamazoo, Grand Rapids, or Detroit. We were headed to Vancouver, Canada and our travel arrangements took us through Minneapolis, where we had a long layover. I was traveling on business, a seven-day trip. Several days prior I made the decision to rearrange my schedule and leave a day earlier than originally planned. Doubt about a vendor's performance was the reason for the change in schedule. My early arrival would provide ample time to make sure all uncertainties were worked through and addressed. I prefer to be proactive in such matters rather than take a *lets-wait-and-see* approach.

One of the perks of my job was the opportunity to bring my wife and children on certain trips. My costs were fixed and were thus legitimate business expenses - travel, hotel, car rental. The additional costs of family travel were minimal. I was personally obligated to pay my family's travel expenses - airlines and meals - and they would arrange entertainment on their own while I was at work. This was still an exceptional benefit that we'd avail ourselves of one, maybe two times a year. I spent about 80 days a year on the road, and I appreciated this benefit. My wife and I had never been to Vancouver so we opted for her to join me on this trip.

Minneapolis is one of our favorite airports to fly through and we often set travel plans to use it for connector flights. The airport's schedules for arrivals and departures seem to fit ours, and I don't recall ever experiencing any significant delays. As an added benefit, the airport concourse has plenty of shops to wander through along with an array of great restaurants. If you are in a hurry you can find a relatively inexpensive sandwich shop and get a meal to go. If you feel like spending a lot of money on fine dining you have options for that as well. On this particular trip our flight arrived late morning and departure wasn't until mid-afternoon so we had plenty of time to wander, eat, and enjoy.

As time approached for our flight to leave we went through check in, walked down the jetway, and boarded the plane. We worked our way down the aisle and found our assigned seats: 3 across; she in the middle, me with the aisle seat. The window seat's occupant had boarded earlier, a good looking guy, trim, clean shaven, blue jeans, golf shirt, baseball cap. "**1**," was embroidered above the bill on front of the cap. Our seat mate acknowledge our presence, nodded, and smiled. I smiled back and asked: "What were you doing in Onekama (pronounced O ne' ka ma)?" If you really want to fracture the pronunciation though you can call it "**1**,".

Onekama is a small town located in the Northwest section of Michigan's Lower Peninsula. It is situated on the eastern shore of Lake Michigan, which automatically qualifies it as one of the prettiest places in the universe: beautiful sunsets, long expansive sandy beaches, and clean, fresh water. (All of you who prefer the ocean, please take note: Lake Michigan may get cold, but it is unsalted and oil free, and there is nothing in there that will eat you.) There is also a world-class golf course nearby. Many who love to golf and aren't put off by three-digit greens fees acknowledge it as a must-visit-at-least-once-in-your-lifetime destination spot. The only drawback to the area is that there is no direct route to get there. One expressway stops about an hour south of Onekama, and another lies two hours east. Consequently there aren't many hotels in the area, nor are there many restaurants. Some do not consider those to be negative points as it does limit the number of folks who even know the place exists, let along go there.

We had a picture-perfect day for flying. The sky was clear with the sun shining brightly, and there were no weather systems forming that would assault the plane and create turbulence. Our seat mate turned out to be quite a nice fellow, pleasant and a good conversationalist. In answer to my original question he explained that he was from Canada and worked in the timber industry. His employer had sent him to a seminar in downstate

Michigan; following the work portion of the seminar two days of golf were included at the aforementioned course. His "**1,**" baseball cap was one of the souvenirs he was bringing home.

The fellow told us a lot about the timber industry. He explained that lumber is a major export for his country and that the United States is Canada's largest trading partner. He also said there were always ongoing negotiations between the two countries regarding pricing, delivery, and forest management. With no animosity he made a statement that stuck in my mind. What he said was that the U.S. and Canada were, in theory, equal trading partners. But in reality the U.S economy is ten times the size of Canada's, so in negotiations the U.S. would say (whatever) and Canada would say OK. There were no real negotiations. The U.S. counterparts always maneuvered for what most benefitted them. I appreciated his candor, yet I found it disturbing that we would abuse the friendship with our *neighbor to the North* in such a manner.

Upon arrival in Vancouver we had to go through Customs. Many well-seasoned travelers were complaining because things were congested and it took a long time. We knew no better, so we just took it in stride and proceeded as part of the slow moving line.

Ah, those were the days! My company provided logistics support for a large corporation, and we were expected to be close by to attend to any details that cropped up. When traveling, wherever they stayed, we stayed. Thus our accommodations in Vancouver were in the nicest hotel I had ever stayed in. Our room was an upper-floor suite located across the street from the Port of Vancouver pier.

After checking in we roamed around the area, decided on a place to eat dinner, and eventually found our way back to the hotel. After a long day of travel we fell asleep.

Weather-wise the next day was as pleasant as the one prior: blue sky, sunshine, warm weather. One thing occurred overnight that we were not aware of. When we awoke in the morning and opened the drapes to look out on the harbor, we found ourselves looking at a ship that had come into port while we slept. We hadn't realized that the pier is where the Alaskan cruise ships dock. There we were though, looking across the way at the crew on the ship's bridge. That is not a common angle from which one typically views a ship. It was such a large ship it stretched from horizon to horizon... OK, that's not quite true. It was a big ship though, and it did fill the full width of our picture window.

I wanted to get to work early, so I got ready and left. My wife had professional journals to read, and sat down at the desk to attend to her day's planned activity.

By late morning I had the work issues resolved and went to find my wife to go to lunch. Back at the hotel she was still reading her journals, but she was also ready for a break. Before heading out I decided to call my office to check on folks back home. The time was about 12:00 PM Pacific time, 3:00 PM Eastern Standard time; the date was September 11, 2001. About six hours earlier the world as we knew it had changed and until that moment I knew nothing about that day's horrific events. All the evil perpetrated by 19 men had been wrought, all the damage done. 2,996 people who started the day alive were now dead. To this day that thought still sobers me!

To this day I also remain impressed and humbled by Canada's response to our national tragedy. Everything the United States did to assume a defensive posture, Canada did to protect our northern border. Sea ports were closed, air space was shut down, borders were secured, and the investigations commenced. Canada treated our loss as their loss. Individuals expressed compassion as well. Every day we remained in Canada, three more than originally planned since the borders were closed, someone said: "We are so sorry for your loss. Let us buy you dinner." How gracious of them! Even the hotel extended empathy and cut our bill by 25%. No one had to do any of that, but they did as an empathetic act of compassion.

The activities that required me to be in Vancouver proceeded, but on a severely truncated scale. A function that was supposed to host 6,000 - 8,000 people had perhaps 1,500 in attendance. Subsequently I had plenty of time, and not a lot of obligations. My wife and I occupied much of our time by meeting people and finding out about their lives. People tend to be talkative and introspective as they cope with evil on the scale of what had just occurred. My wife and I like to know what people think, and in that environment our inquisitive nature benefitted others by giving them someone to talk to. When the opportunity arose we'd ask our Canadian hosts about their experiences with U.S. relations. What the timber industry fella told us on our flight in was unsettling to us and we wanted to hear what others had to say. They told similar stories.

Over the years I've thought of the events just described, concentrating on relationships and perspectives instead of the other things we all remember so well. I keep thinking what a stark contrast exists between the perception foreigners have of self-absorbed Americans, and how the Canadians responded on September 11 with empathy. The issue goes deeper than U.S. foreign policy (which in my opinion has always stunk) and comes down to a personal level. What we think of ourselves, and how we treat others, is the crux of the matter.

At this point I'm looking for a witty way to end this essay, but it's not working very well. I find myself thinking about a myriad of issues that deal with the dynamics of a "have it your way" society. Those thoughts may take me into the subject for another essay so I won't delve further at this point. Instead let me get back to the completion of this essay.

My first thought for closure was to write three bullets:
- We have created a monster and it is us.
- Most people are either clueless or unappreciative about the abundance of blessing we have in the USA. Gratitude is generally not in our lexicon.
- We are in trouble.

While there is truth and merit in those statements, that would be a cop-out ending. Besides it doesn't tell the whole truth. Those statements apply to many Americans, but not to every American.

I recently returned from an overseas trip where I encountered people from many walks of life and of many different national origins. My observations reminded me that people are people regardless of where they come from. Some are pleasant, some are rude. On the whole, many who hail from the North American continent bring with them a moral base that compels them to be polite and respectful. That makes them susceptible to scammers, scoundrels, and pickpockets who desire to relieve them of their possessions. Our rules of order do not necessarily align with other peoples' rules of order. Some of those whom I encountered who hail from places elsewhere raise rude behavior to a whole new art form. It is the world in which they live.

Let's close by taking things from the macro and reducing them to the micro. For the moment disregard societal values and focus on the individual - you; me. Most of us will never be in a position where we can change society on a grand scale, but we can decide how we want to live, and by what standards of conduct we will behave. Here are two standards that I believe are worth keeping in mind:

> The *Golden Rule* applies: "Treat others as you want them to treat you."
> So does Teddy Roosevelt's admonition: "Walk softly, and carry a big stick."

Be polite; don't be stupid. Through all, don't miss the opportunity to edify others. In the long run you will get back more than you give.

The key lesson I hoped to convey here is: <u>Know who your friends are and appreciate them, in word and in action.</u>

Everyone is My Superior

Have you heard it said: God gave you two ears and one mouth and they should be used in those proportions(?) I don't know when I first heard that adage. Perhaps my parents used it as a polite way to tell me to shut up. It is a good rule to keep in mind though. Listen much and speak little is another way to say the same thing.

"Better to keep your mouth shut and let people think you are a fool than open it and confirm their suspicions" is a quote attributed to both Abraham Lincoln and Mark Twain. These words express the same point. With humorous intent, whoever it was that said it actually used a rough paraphrase of a passage from the Bible.[8] That source is used as the basis of many quotable phrases.

The admonition can be offerer and received in either a negative or a positive manner. Offense may be appropriate if the statement is made in terms of someone telling you what you have to say is not important. In that context the words are used as a put-down, an insult. Under those terms the words may be taken as a challenge to a person's self-worth. I would take offense, as would many others, if the statement was made with such intent. So as not to misconstrue the speakers purpose, one's reaction should be evaluated based on whom it is that said the words, and what the nature of the relationship is; an assessment of the level of respect that exists between the two parties.

---

[8] Proverbs 17:28 reads: Even a fool is thought wise if he keeps silent, and discerning if he holds his tongue. (NIV)

I think it best to view the admonition in a positive context. The phrase can be offered as words of encouragement with another's best interest in mind. "God gave you two ears and one mouth" is a concise way of saying: "Pay attention; listen to what others have to tell you. You have an opportunity to learn and this will benefit you." Though my initial reaction may be less than positive - pride tends to get in the way for all of us - I cannot be offended by anyone who is willing to express something that is in my best interest. That is a mark of friendship. I like being around others who are concerned about me. I appreciate the opportunities to learn something new, and I appreciate things that will benefit me.

For that reason there is value in looking at these situations through a positive light. Maybe the things I learn will enable me to earn more money or enable me to work less so I can engage in other pursuits. Maybe the things I learn will enable me to help others or lessen the anxieties attached to undesirable situations I have to contend with. The possibility of those outcomes are all good. I want to seize any opportunity that offers those benefits.

Without any real forethought or planning I fell into the practice of listening and learning soon after graduation from college. I was hired to be the site engineer on a large construction project and until my first day of work I had never stepped foot on a construction site. I may have known a lot about design and engineering, but the real education was about to begin.

By my position I was, technically, second in command on the worksite and I figured I needed to learn construction methods and procedures fast. The best way to do that, I reasoned, was to ask craftsmen why they were doing things in certain ways as I watched them go about their duties.

Though I may have many shortcomings one I am not limited by is to hold my level of education over someone less educated. I believe in the value of education, but experience takes precedence over book learning every day. Thus I was not inhibited to talk with craftsmen and learn what I could of their skills. Plumbers taught me to sweat pipes, and electricians taught me how to do their trade without getting electrocuted (high on my priority list). I even learned from unskilled laborers.

"Unskilled" is a common term, but it is a misnomer. Along with other tasks laborers are the guys who pour concrete, and with that, there are tricks of the trade you need to know. For example, concrete poured into tall walls or thick slabs needs to be vibrated to assure proper consolidation and the elimination of voids. Insufficient vibration results in voids not being fully removed, which then necessitates expensive repairs. Excessive vibration can cause concrete formwork to blow apart. You then have a nightmare with concrete going places you didn't intend it to go. This can be problematic and potentially dangerous. Better to learn the proper techniques from someone who possesses the knowledge rather than learn the hard way.

The same held true for members of other construction trades. Pipe fitters, millwrights, and operating engineers all knew more about their respective trades than did I. Even painters taught me a lot. Note: Anyone can hold a paintbrush but not everyone holding a paintbrush is a painter. There is a distinction.

I have fond memories of getting to "talk shop" with trades people; the opportunities I had to learn things I would not otherwise know. Usually my inquiries on basic matters would lead the craftsmen to tell me other techniques of their trades. I thought this was great, as it furthered my knowledge. Occasionally I'd run into some dufus who would refuse to tell me anything saying I would then take his job. I'd respond by saying that I didn't want his job as I already made more money than he, then I'd move on and simply ask the next guy.

Sometimes I'd run into guys who, by all outward appearance, were dumber than a box of dirt. Yet they were good craftsmen. It occurred to me that if they were proficient in their skills, I too could develop the same. Procedures and methodology I learned long ago have benefited me through the years. A free education (hooray!), psychologically made all the better by it coming from people whom others may look down on.

So this essay is written as a tribute to the many people from whom I have learned over the years. The title is an acknowledgement of my appreciation for what they taught me and how I benefitted from their instruction.

<u>Everyone is my superior in at least one capacity</u>. I have learned much from many.

I have benefitted greatly from this quest to learn from others. I learned about Bar-B-Que from a guy named Booker. (His is the best in the universe, I might add; or at least it's the best I have tasted thus far.) Another good man, a recovering heroin addict, taught me how to keep mosquitos from bothering me when working on scaffolding. (Heroin addicts who have turned their lives around will always tell you they are "recovering". They will not use the word past-tense.) Other people taught me about gun safety, tig welding, and proper techniques for weight lifting. Regardless of which of us has the highest IQ or the more extensive education, each of those people know more than I do in at least one capacity, their area of expertise. So in that capacity they are my superior.

The opportunity to learn from others is vast, and being the recipient of such education can be rewarding. Professional people whom I know - doctors, dentists, lawyers - have taught me, as have business people and their employees. Others have done the same in different subject areas: Chris, someone I met recently, gave me a crash course in finances related to the broadcast industry; my friend John, a walking dictionary, is a huge source of information who also possesses the knowledge to tie Biblical facts to the evidence provided through secular history. Each one is my superior in at least one capacity.

This thought struck me as humorous: Death, when it comes, will be very inconvenient. When I die it will be my time to die, but I will still have a lot to learn from others.

There is another aspect of this method of learning from others that I value. It is the opportunity to instill confidence in others and propel them in a positive direction as they progress through life. Providing others the opportunity to speak on something they are familiar with may also build confidence in other areas of their lives.

In 1936 a man named Dale Carnegie wrote a book titled <u>How to Win Friends and Influence People</u>. The book came out of a study conducted by the author, whereby he sought to understand what attributes successful people possess. The book is considered a classic, a must read, for many business school curriculums. It is still popular more than 75 years after it was first published.

One point cited in the book addresses the discomfort many people feel when talking with strangers. The fear of initiating a conversation, and the threats of lapses in the flow - long quiet periods - seem overwhelming. These fears cause people to withdraw, the awkwardness of isolation being preferred to the awkwardness of clunky conversations. Though natural, this results in missed opportunities to learn something new. Carnegie's recommended solution to this problem is to get others to talk about themselves. This works. "Talk to someone about themselves, and they'll listen for hours" is a quote from the book.

At social gatherings I enjoy seeking out the most awkward appearing person and striking up a conversation with them. My assumption is that they appear awkward because they feel uncomfortable. Perhaps they don't know anyone in the gathering, or there is some other aspect they find intimidating. Safe questions to ask are: "What is their name; where did they go to school; have they always lived in the area; what brought them to the meeting"... things like that. Start the conversation, then let it flow. Gaps and moment of quiet are allowed.

Conversely, starting a conversation with work or family related questions isn't usually the best place to begin. There may be unsettled issues that the person doesn't want to reveal. A conversation may naturally flow in that direction, but a smooth flowing conversation is less likely to begin there. The secret is to get others to talk about themselves. Do this, and express interest in what they have to say. They, in turn, will think you are a brilliant conversationalist. In reality you will have said very little and they will have done most of the talking. You, in the meantime, may have the opportunity to learn something new.

This "secret", I am certain, is what got me into a competitive graduate school program. During a personal interview that was part of the university's admission procedure I simply asked a few questions of the program director and got him talking about his business experiences. Through my one-hour interview I probably did no more than 10 minutes of talking.

My friends Cliff and Mary became my mentors in learning to carry on conversations with others. Their ability to get people to talk about themselves is an admirable quality they shared. A genuine interest in the well-being of others compelled them, so they would masterfully steer conversations in that direction. Even with established relationships they orchestrated conversations so they spent more time listening than they did talking. Most folks obliged willingly.

Following one occasion my wife and I realized that we had dominated a conversation without meaning to do so. We told Cliff and Mary a lot about our thoughts, but heard little in reply. That is how they wanted it. They were about fifteen years older than us so they knew the challenges we would face being newly married. They demonstrated their concern by letting us talk, and commented only enough to steer us in a direction they knew we should go. I hold these folks in the highest esteem.

It then become a game for us, a challenge. Out of a genuine reciprocal of care my wife and I would try to get Cliff and Mary to talk about themselves. Maybe the balance of conversation shifted a little, but they were the masters, and always succeeded in getting us to be the ones talking. We never caught on when the shift occurred.

Such was Cliff and Mary's nature, to express their concerns for others in this manner. They won many friends, and influenced many people.

Cliff died several years ago after a long battle against cancer. By that time he and Mary were living in Colorado. Cliff's funeral was podcast over the internet for the benefit of those of us scattered across North America, and perhaps the world, who could not be there in person to say goodbye to our friend.

Cliff and Mary will always be my superiors. They are people I want to emulate.

The Path Through Life I – Meteoric Ascents and Misfortunes

The option was presented, though I don't know the extent to which another choice would truly be considered. At the time I wondered whether the question was asked because our opinion might influence the outcome, or if it was just put out there to stroke our egos. I don't like to sound cynical but I don't want to be ignorant in matters driven by human nature either. We were, after all, an *Executive Class*, and there is always benefit in stroking executives' egos, or so goes the expressed thinking of many.

The time for graduation was approaching. As a class we were asked whom we would like to have as the university's commencement speaker. The top choice of most was a prominent New York real estate developer who had recently been the subject of many headlines. I am sure their thinking was, if given the opportunity, the guy could talk about his accomplishments and pass on key points of information that we, soon to be MBA graduates, could take forth into our careers. I wasn't particularly keen on the idea of choosing this guy because I figured his ego would get in the way and we would have to endure the ramblings of him patting himself on the back. A different guy received my nomination for commencement speaker. My choice had also been the topic of news headlines, though for a less desirable reason. John Connelly, a man with vast and lengthy credentials, a man well regarded by many, both individuals and the corporate business community, had filed for personal bankruptcy.

By my line of thinking the New York guy would tell us what worked well for him and avoid commenting on the deals that didn't go so well. I assumed his pride would make it difficult to talk about those events. In contrast, Mr. Connelly's pride had already been stripped away. I hoped he might talk about where he lost track of key details, how events and timing worked against him, and how variables over which we have no control but must be mindful of could likewise work against us if we lost our focus and abandoned prudent judgement.

I thought this would be a fitting sendoff from graduate school, a last lesson. The logic behind my rationale was that it is easy to dream and think about the upside, something we naturally do when we hear others talk about their success, but it is prudent to pay attention to the downside lest we make ourselves vulnerable to failure. Learn to "float a boat and see how many holes you can shoot in it before it sinks" is metaphorically how one person I know terms this. If the boat doesn't sink you know you have a good idea, but don't assume the boat won't sink without first trying to sink it.

John Connelly, a successful and adept politician, gained national prominence on November 22, 1963. As governor of Texas he rode that day in a motorcade as it wove its way through Dallas Texas. As the procession passed through an area known as Dealey Plaza a better-known politician sitting in the back seat, President of the United States John F. Kennedy, was assassinated. Though not a target of the assassination, Connelly was seriously wounded in the shooting.

Connelly recovered from his wounds, and his political career continued. In 1980 he vied to become the candidate of choice for the upcoming presidential elections that were to be held later that year. Through the primary election process he concluded there were other candidates more popular and better known than he, so he withdrew from the competition and retired into a private legal practice.

John Connelly's wealth grew. At one point his net worth was three million dollars - investments, cash in the bank, and no debt; the type of stuff you can live a lifetime off of and never run out of money. As a well-regarded corporate attorney his cash flow was equally large. He also sat on the Board of Directors for several large corporations. Suffice it to say he made a lot of money.

With the rapidly expanding economy of the1980s, however, there was plenty more money to be made. Building on a long history and extensive experience in real estate, Mr. Connelly took on debt and invested as a real estate developer. His net worth soared from $3 million to an estimated $54 million. His empire grew faster than the economy though. He got over extended, was unable to pay his debts as obligated, and went into default. At age 69 Gov. John B. Connelly (ret.) filed personal bankruptcy.

What a roller coaster ride:
- From a net worth of $3 million (cash in the bank), to $54 million (estimated) with a lot of risk, to $17 million in debt
- From reality, to fantasy, to reality
- From rising star to has-been
- From pride to humility.

As I recall, Mr. Connelly acknowledged his failings and went through the humiliations with grace. He accepted fault and did not try to blame others. His fall didn't leave him as a pauper, though the prestige and extreme affluence he once enjoyed were gone for good.

There are similar stories of others that could be told. Billy Durant, the founder of General Motors Corporation is one name that comes to mind. He lost his fortune as a result of the stock market crash of 1929 and lived out his days as the manager of a bowling alley.

Think for a moment what lessons might be learned from those who have enjoyed phenomenal success, then experienced an even larger magnitude of loss. Those who maintain dignity and grace while enduring a humbling process may be some of the best teachers we can find.

There are also those who go through a gain-and-loss experience, but find reasons to blame others for their misfortunes. Their pride keeps them from admitting what other people already know.

Isn't pride interesting? We like to think of it as a good thing, our measure of personal accountability. We nod our heads in affirmation of taking pride in a job well done, or as a craftsman of taking pride in one's workmanship. Yet it is also pride that blinds us to that which others may so readily see.

There is a saying: "Pride comes before a fall." That which we strive for, believing it to be good, may be the thing that destroys us. In reality pride is just a form of self-adulation, us getting caught up in ourselves.

Perhaps humility is a better virtue than pride. Let others acknowledge our accomplishments if there are accomplishments to be acknowledged. Instead of pride, perhaps our focus should be on developing a sense of gratitude, a sense of humility and gratefulness that we possess whatever abilities are needed for the respective accomplishments that others appreciate.

Take a moment and think about this. Think of prideful (pride filled) people whom you know, and think of humble people whom you know. Which group is the most fatiguing; which is the more enjoyable to be around?

There is much that you can learn from other people's experiences. Given the possible outcome of some situations that is the preferred option. The alternative is that you have to endure the hard lessons and resultantly painful obligations yourself.

'nuff said.

The Path Through Life II - Trepidations and Foggy Notions

Peace of mind seems like a gift everyone wants but many miss. I don't know how to give it to others; I don't know how anyone can give it to me, though I wish they could. Is it an elusive gift from God or is it a gift we give ourselves?

Here is one of those soul searching questions that beg answer. Why is it that peace, genuine inner peace, is something we crave but seldom find? It seems at best that it comes and goes, sometimes it doesn't come at all.

Maybe the answer lies in the subject of the dependent clause and attached verb - we crave. In the singular we becomes I, and now the matter is more accurately stated: I crave. I am looking for something that will satisfy longings and give purpose; something that will abate frustrations, or that will silence the demons of doubt. I wonder, in our quest for this intangible, if we unknowingly shape our character?

How do we find peace of mind? I can think of three outcomes to this pursuit with two of them not being good.

I.   If we allow the longing to overwhelm us we get beat down and never satisfy the question. Perhaps that leads to frustration, fatigue, and timidity. One becomes downcast, outwardly an emotionally numb pauper whose life exhibits mostly sorrow and little joy. While appearing outwardly benign there may be a fomenting torrent building within that other people do not see. Maybe this is the cause of rage some people harbor that plant the seeds for baseless destruction and much sorrow. This is not a good option.

II.   If we disregard the quest we become callous and hollow, maybe even demanding and mean. Don't allow oneself to suffer the pain and hurt that accompanies the desire. The result may be that these folks become desensitized to pain and hurt. This is not a good option either.

III. Or we can pursue the quest and seek a solution. Understand that it is a quest, sometimes frustrating, but also a journey of discovery, and not an insurmountable obstacle. I'm kinda thinking there is something to be gained here.

This may be a nonissue for many because they choose to make it so. They choose to live shallow lives and not confront matters of character, perhaps because no one else matters as much as they matter.

That statement sounds more harsh than it needs to. Maybe for some people this is a nonissue, simply because it is a nonissue. Perhaps they just don't think about things like this. Such an exercise of introspection may be a completely foreign idea to them. That is OK, I guess. Let people live their lives as they so choose.

For those of us who do seek answers though, the basis of our pursuit is to seek a fullness of life in the individual context of however that is defined. We intentionally make ourselves vulnerable as a necessary part of a learning process.

With the latter choice there is an education process we are subject to. The lessons learned can come fast, or the process can be slow and arduous. The option is ours. Either we learn to prioritize our thoughts and hold onto certain foundational truths, or we fluctuate between moments of confidence and self-doubt.

I must be a slow learner, for it seems I often land in the second category. One benefit of this default category though, is the affirmations that come with reminders that I am not alone in attacking these psychologies.

Here is a current example of my concern: As I write I sometimes question both the value and motivation of this book. Will I be able to adequately address issues everyone contends with and help others in their pursuits as I desire, or will these words just come across as the ramblings of some clown with an abnormal thought process? Am I writing and exposing the struggles of my soul so others may know they are not alone, or is this just a cathartic attempt to let go of whatever it is I need to let go of?

The answers to the first question can't be fully known, so I don't need to spend much time pondering that. Check your motives, do what you can, move forward, and let go. That seems to be a good rule to live by. Yes is the short answer to the second question. Perhaps both conditions apply. I can then expand that by reasserting the rule mentioned a moment ago. So, let go; let's go.

If you are interested in knowing what it is that makes you tick and what it is that you value, this is a quest worth undertaking. You may discover things about yourself you never before realized. You may realize you are holding onto baggage you really ought to let go of. If the process proves too painful there is an emergency exit. You can quit at any time, pick up the baggage you discarded earlier, and resume doing that which you have always done. That is not my preference though. It is more my curiosity to move forward and see what I can discover about myself. If it's good, great; if it's bad, then once it's identified I can deal with it. A win-win situation for me, yay!

I am reminded of a story I heard many years ago, one I keep at the forefront of my mind. It is real life, not completely positive, but one with a satisfying ending. It keeps my line of thinking on the proper track. It offers encouragement and generates hope.

Before continuing further it is worth taking a detour to comment on that key word, hope. I have come to realize there are two ways to think of the word. One way is beneficial, the other folly. One hope is to have complete confidence in the occurrence of something yet unseen, or that something will happen that has not yet happened. This isn't a baseless hope. What it implies is that you strongly believe something will occur because you know a lot about other related details. The confidence comes with things you already know to be true. Hope of this nature is well placed. There is a foundation of support that justifies its existence. This hope, however, demands discipline: Discipline to be calm when your mind wants to rage; discipline to keep moving when you feel like giving up; discipline to tell the demons of doubt to be quiet.

The other hope is just wishful thinking. Perhaps it is innocuous: "I hope tomorrow will be sunny"; or not so innocuous, the mantra of an unproven politician. At best this hope is inconsequential. If the day is sunny, great. If not, we adapt because we know every day can't be sunny. Putting "hope" in more extreme matters of this nature, though, is foolish. It is an attempted escape from reality and responsibility, one that will not succeed.

This story offers hope of a positive nature.

The man who told the story was in his late 60s and he was the CEO of a family owned business. At the time of our meeting the company's annual sales were around eight hundred million dollars. He was the second generation, have taken over from his father years earlier. The company was now entering its next phase, with the third generation assuming top management responsibility in a planned and controlled manner. His time for retirement was not far off and he was looking forward to the change. The man had worked hard to build the business as had other family members and a slew of trusted employees. All would soon be rewarded handsomely for their effort and commitment. The story being told was that of how the company was founded, and grew through the years, always profitable.

The founder of the business, the CEO's father, came out of corporate America where he was one of the captains of industry for his time. In the 1920s the father was earning a hundred thousand dollars a year as his salary, the equivalent of a large multimillion dollar income today. Yet he was dissatisfied with his position. His goal was to start a business that could be passed on to his sons and future generations. Acting on this desire the man quit his job and started the company he had planned for. I don't recall many of the details, perhaps few were provided, but the business did not go well. After a relatively short existence, several years perhaps, the company collapsed and ended in bankruptcy.

The man's fall was precipitous. Gone was the wealth, affluence and accolades that accompanied his earlier successes; shame and humiliation were now his companions. Dejected and seemingly alone the man decided to commit suicide by smashing his expensive automobile into a bridge abutment. That did not go well either. He survived.

This is not the type of story often told, and that is a shame. Most success stories have a dark side associated with them, and it is through adversity that you learn best. Those are the stories of substance that convey lessons of value: the ability to overcome adversity; perseverance; learning to say you are sorry; humility; and more. They challenge you to stay focused when your inclination is to give up. They keep your mind from going to the dark side.

The man convalesced and was committed to a sanitarium, an insane asylum is the less polite name, and was treated by the doctors for what they considered to be a mental condition.

As the CEO told the story he stressed a key point: Hard, physical labor was a core component of the treatment regimen his father was subject to. The labor wasn't mandated as punishment, rather it provided the physical evidence of accomplishment, the opportunity to say: "Look what I did today." Sometimes the purpose of assigned labor was obvious, gardening to provide vegetables for the sanitarium's kitchen, sometimes the purpose was not so obvious. The labor was an important component of the treatment plan though. It was an integral part of the process meant to get the man back on track and instill a sense of worth and confidence.

Over time the father recovered and was discharged from the sanitarium. He recommenced the pursuit of his goal and developed a business that could be passed on to his children. The second attempt worked quite well.

The CEO closed the story by repeating a phrase he often heard from his father: "Work's a blessing." From lessons learned during his time in the sanitarium the father believed in the value of hard, physical work to build confidence and develop a sense of accomplishment. He believed too, that it taught him to think through problems, prioritize obligations, and develop solutions. Therein, he found peace.

That is a great story. It provides a framework for accomplishment that anyone can follow. It validate the notion that there are both physical and mental elements that contribute to finding inner peace. It is not just a mental exercise. The physical application cuts through the agitation that often accompanies unsettledness.

There is also an unspoken component of the treatment plan that ran through the story and was very much a part of the father's recover. It came about by the father learning to think on a broader scale and not get overwhelmed by the burdens of the day. That was the objective, and the physical labor set the environment in which he could learn. His mind was engaged in the process of analyzing, thinking, assessing, and coming up with solutions to matters that troubled him as he employed his muscles to accomplish the physical task at hand. It also gave him the chance to consider those things he could accomplish, and those things that were beyond his reach. Through this he developed an appreciation for a simple passage from the Bible that reads: "Be still, and know that I am God."[9] Maybe that is an appreciation that can benefit us too.

Peace at last.

---

[9]   Psalm 46:10

Table Manners

"Don't meet your food halfway" is an admonition that belongs in the Admonition Hall of Fame, if such a place were to exist. It is a phrase used by a friend who runs a children's day-care whose intent is to teach those in her charge proper table manners. In this case specifically her instruction is when sitting at a table, bring the food up to your mouth, don't bring your mouth down to the food. That is her most creative phrase, but it is used in concert with a litany of others meant to teach children how not to look like a slob. Keep your elbows off the table; sit with your back straight; don't talk with food in your mouth; chew with your mouth closed; hold your fork properly; and a host of other phrases are used as instruction for the children's development.

My friend is both a good day-care provider and a good mother. In both capacities she is concerned for the well-being of those in her charge. She knows that how people present themselves will influence the opportunities they have in life. As it pertains to her children, she wants them to succeed. Instructing the slovenliness out of them will help them on their way. Her instructions start at an early age.

I commend my friend whenever I watch someone who didn't learn those lessons. I don't mean to come across as being snooty. My concern is as much for their benefit as it is a reaction to something I find distasteful. There is nothing objectionable about advancing the social graces, nor is it wrong to desire that folks show their best side. I do, after all, hope for the best for people, and I delight in seeing others express discipline in their lives by how they present themselves. I also know that others are watching, and the opportunities that come someone's way can be advanced or thwarted based on that very same thing, how they present themselves.

The fact that people are watching can bring up a whole discussion in itself. Some may say: I don't care what other's think of me and I'm going to live however I so please. I'm fine with that, and I don't want people to pretend to be something they aren't. I'm not asking for disingenuousness, yet I would ask: Why would you want to shortchange yourself; why set out intentionally to miss opportunities? Why would you give someone who has something of value to offer you a reason to write you off before you have the chance to prove yourself? A lack of concern for social graces may work against you in that very manner.

Some may say: People should not be judgmental, to which I would reply: People are judgmental. It's part of our protection mechanism, and if you say you don't judge others you are either delusional, a liar or a fool. I am not advocating condescending behavior, nor am I promoting class distinctions. I am merely making a statement of fact: We do judge others and others judge us. It is part of our natural instinct. It serves as the preliminary assessment of any situation we may find ourselves in, and collectively, it defines the core values of the communities in which we desire to live.

These essays are meant to be positive and encouraging, though I don't want them to be Polly Anna-esque (sugarcoated) in their presentation. Simply stated, be aware that people are watching. They are assessing how you carry yourself and how you handle various situations.

As people conduct their assessments they may be looking deeper to determine your core values, the rules of conduct by which you choose to live your life. If anyone is watching you that closely they may have something to offer, something you esteem or identify as valuable. Those who are watching also want to make sure their trust in you, if extended, is well placed. I saw such an event play out in a magnanimous way.

I have a friend whom I have known for as long as I can remember. He's one of my closest friends though I don't get to see him very often. He now lives in a different part of the country and we stay in contact through e-mails and regular phone conversations.

Recently my friend called from Seattle, where he had flown that day for an Executive Committee meeting for his company. His career has taken off over the past five years, and it is exciting to see how he handles the trust his company expresses in him. He has proven himself capable, competent, and dutiful, and in so doing now gets to enjoy the accoutrements of success that come with a job well done. Things were not always that way though.

Prior to this time my friend's career was languishing. His position of employment wasn't bad, neither in terms of accomplishment nor in his ability to provide for his family, but opportunities to excel seemed fleeting. My friend didn't need the affirmation some crave with a job title, yet much of his talent was sitting idle.

The company my friend now works for first met him years ago on a project he terms as small scale and insignificant. My friend's employer at the time had made promises that had not been honored. He stepped in to ensure that promises made were promises kept. Unbeknownst to my friend, people were watching.

These are the hallmarks of my friend: dutiful, responsible behavior; honesty; an unwavering commitment to integrity. If you ask him though he'll just give a humble reply saying he strives to do the right thing, whatever that may be.

A significant amount of time passed, but the memory of my friend's actions were lodged in someone's mind, someone with clout and influence. When a situation arose that required hiring a responsible person who possessed integrity and a breadth of talents, that someone in the company he now works for remembered my friend's name from long ago. Seemingly innocuous actions paid off in a big way, and doors of opportunity opened in ways that could not be foreseen. For my friend, and those of us who revel in his success, these are exciting and satisfying times.

For inspiration my friend likes to recite a story about legendary University of Alabama football coach Paul "Bear" Bryant. I'll see if I can get it straight here:

> Bear Bryant was head coach of the Crimson Tide from 1958-1982. One of the responsibilities of his job was to search out and recruit talented high school players who would come play football at Bama. As the newly appointed head coach, one such trip took him through the backroads of the deep south. In 1958 segregation, prejudice, and racism were alive and strong in Alabama.

> One day as lunchtime approached Bryant decided to stop at a particular diner. He, a white man, walked in and sat down at the lunch counter. All conversation came to a halt, and he realized he was in a black-owned establishment that was accustomed to catering only to other black people.

> Rather than make an issue of what, at the time, could be considered a serious faux pas, Bryant simply asked the proprietor for the luncheon special. The proprietor, knowing his fare was "black-folks" food, not "white-folks" food responded by saying the luncheon special is chitlins, do you know what they are? Bryant's response was something to the effect of: "I was raised in Arkansas and I've had miles of chitlins, but I've never tried yours and I would like to." (Chitlins are pig intestines.) Bryant's disarming statement opened the door for conversation about football and talented local players. As he paid his bill and prepared to leave the restaurant owner asked Bryant to send him one of his publicity picture as the new coach, saying he wanted to hang it in his diner. Bryant obliged and sent a signed photograph upon his return to campus. Through the years Bryant would stop at that diner when scouting trips took him nearby. Bryant and the proprietor would renew their conversations.

For the first 12 years of Bryant's tenure at Alabama blacks were not recruited to play football. By Bryant's admission he did not feel the attitudes of the time would accommodate such action. During that time though, when Bryant found a talented black player, he would let other college coaches know of the potential recruit. Coach "Muddy" Waters of Michigan State University was a recipient of such favors. Times and attitudes did change, however, and Alabama actively started recruiting black players for its sports programs in 1971.

Late in Bryant's career there was one black football player he desperately wanted to recruit, but the player instead pledged to a different university's program. Several days following the announcement though, the player called Bryant and asked if a scholarship opportunity was still available at Alabama. If so the player said he would like to play for Bryant. Coach Bryant said those arrangements could be worked out, but asked what brought about the change in the player's decision? The young man explained that when he informed his grandfather of his decision, the grandfather in no uncertain terms, and with the authority that only a family patriarch can command, told his grandson the <u>only</u> college coach he could play for was Bear Bryant. <u>No further discussion would be allowed on the matter</u>. The grandfather, it turned out, was the diner owner to whom Bryant had sent the picture long ago. That picture still hung on the wall of the grandfather's restaurant.

As Bryant finished telling the story he concluded by saying he didn't do anything special, he only did the right thing.

As it turns out, people were watching Bear Bryant, too.

A quote of Bear Bryant's is worth keeping in mind: "It's not the will to win that matters, everyone has that. It's the will to prepare to win that matters."

So as you go forward and exercise your will to prepare to win, keep your table manners in mind. I can promise they'll contribute to your success, because I know that people are watching. Just as it has for my friend, and just as it did for Bear Bryant, doing the right thing may pay off for you in ways you cannot imagine.

Do the right thing even when (you think) no one is watching. That sounds like the definition of integrity to me.

The Daily Challenges of Grace -
Granting and Receiving

Granting and receiving grace, being willing to forgive the minor slights and serious affronts that others have directed toward me and being willing to accept the fact that some people have decided to not hold me liable for wrongs I have committed... Wow, this topic for consideration is not for the faint of heart.

I don't very often hear people talk about grace, so it must not be a word used in our everyday vernacular. Its absence may imply that for a large segment of the population it is a totally foreign idea. Does it seem that way to you, or do you get to see grace in action? Perhaps the "bad" that I see in the everyday world just sticks in my mind, or maybe I am just cynical.

As I consider this notion of grace it seems to me that many people's reaction would be something as follows:

> "Grace(?), the heck with you. Why should I forgive someone if they set out to cause me harm - physical, emotional, financial, or otherwise? I know it was intentional, and I have every right to get even. You agree with me, don't you? I'll show them a thing or two!
>
> As for that other part, people not holding me accountable, well I can explain that. Whatever it was wasn't intentional, or at least I didn't mean to get caught. Besides I'm not as bad as some other folks. Think of Pol Pot, or Jeffrey Dalmer,

or that Castro guy who kidnapped the three girls, or any of those other bad people. I'm not like them. Actually, as I think about it, I resent the fact that you accused me. You should forget about this all together because if you don't it may affect our friendship."

If our society chose to get away from what I see as its dominant attitude it would significantly change our culture for the better. It would also put a bunch of lawyers out of work, another change for the better. I kinda like that idea. (The lawyer comment was mostly a joke, but not completely.)

I doubt societal attitudes have ever been fully pleasant and rosy, but things weren't always as negative and caustic as they are now. So when did that change? I spent a fair amount of time thinking about this and realized it wasn't all that long ago.

If you believe that leadership comes from the top I can correlate a significant change and outlook right back to the era of a specific president. After all, leadership does come from the top, and the power of the "bully pulpit"[10] influences everything, starting at the top and working its way from there down.

If U.S. presidents wore jerseys with their respective numbers on them, I'd point to the guy wearing number 42. (Sorry Jackie Robinson, your story is great and your character admirable, so there is no reference to you made here. 42 is just a number you share with someone else.) Also, for those too young to know and those who choose not to remember, a common notion of the time was that we had a Mr. & Mrs. tagteam presidency, so what applies to him equally applies to her.

I'm not here to vilify the guy, a bunch of people love him, but things changed inextricably during his administration. People want to like 42. His (aw shucks) demeanor is engaging and disarming, yet he, his advisors,

---

[10] "Bully pulpit" is a term that was used by President Theodore "Teddy" Roosevelt to describe the power of influence contained in words spoken by the President.

mouthpieces, spouse, and administration were masters at vilifying others and planting innuendos and outright assaults meant to suggest nefarious motives and ill intentions. Grace, and consideration of other points of view, were nowhere to be found. Sadly, the guy who now wears jersey number 44 has pushed this type of conduct to a new low. These are facts, and they genuinely cause me sorrow.

There are some who may want to correct me and say grace left during the campaign of 42's predecessor. Good try, but not so. Lee Atwater, the campaign advisor they credit (or discredit) for their claim doesn't compare to Mr. and Mrs. 42. He didn't attack character or intent, rather perceived ability. Even with that being what some would term as "just politics", Atwater was later compelled to apologize for what he perceived as his transgressions.

This essay is not meant to be a political diatribe, and it certainly doesn't conform to my goal to have lighthearted readings. This does, however, strike me as a critically important issue. How we handle it defines the fabric of our society. The contrast in what we choose is like the contrast between silk and burlap: the former strong, yet pleasingly smooth and soft; the latter may get the job done, but it is coarse, scratchy, and typically dirty. It seems to me that there has been a lot of chaffing going on for quite some time.

If a greater emphasis was placed on grace many of the unsettling ills of our country would abate and subside. It would temper everything from the raging hostilities of political discourse, to road rage, to teenage bullying. Bad and atrocious behavior would be significantly curtailed.

For these reasons we need to take a serious look at the subject of grace and the application of it as a matter of practice.

To have a good foundation to build on let's see how Daniel Webster defines the word *grace* in his dictionary. (The guy was busy.) Webster has 16 options listed, all of which are applicable definitions. Number 6 is the one that best fits - mercy; clemency; pardon.

Those are easy words to say, but often difficult ones to put in place to guide our actions, particularly mercy. So just what does it take to put grace into practice? Not having a great, workable solution let's examine a couple ideas and see where they take us.

A good starting point is to identify factors that may influence the existence of a less-than-desirable situation.

I. Maybe there is an absence of grace because people are scared. When people get scared their self-protection mechanisms kick in and barriers go up. Grace has a hard time competing under those conditions.

    It seems to me that people are scared because of the vast amount of uncertainty that pervades everyday life. Let's face it, institutions that we count on to be stable have failed.

    •   Many institutions of organized religion are either blasé in their adherence to core values, nothing more than a social do-good organization, or grossly hypocritical in the variance of standards between speech and action. Many churches stand up against homosexuality because the Bible condemns such relationships, but they keep quiet about adultery, knowing there are "good" people in the congregation guilty of such acts. Yet the Bible speaks to both. Some churches confuse their commission to reach out to a lost and hurting world with protesting against whatever the perceived social injustice of the day is. More than one television evangelist has preached the value of a monogamous sexual relationship kept within the confines of marriage, only to have their empires collapse when they get caught in bed with a woman who is not their spouse. No wonder so many non-Christians think Christians are hypocritical.
    •   Various levels of government have failed us. So much for "of the people, by the people." In many ways the common perception is "by the select few, for the benefit of the select few." If you consider class distinctions it is easy to see those who run the country sitting on top of the heap, and many of their underlings protected from

actions for which the masses would be held accountable were they guilty of the same.

- Institutions of higher education have failed many. Go to college and get qualified to get a good job; graduate from college with a massive amount of student loan debt and not be able to find a job. What a terrible position to be in when you are just starting out in life on your own.

- The financial system has failed many. Work hard, save for the future, get wiped out financially, and watch as politically connected groups prosper at the expense of others.

- The media has failed us. No longer is news reported in a manner that enables us to evaluate facts and make our own decisions. Very often it is reported with a bias. Those who do not agree risk being ostracized, or worse, vilified if they speak out against the positions of common proclamation. In addition, what is passed on as news is often presented with hysteria and an accusatory overtone attached: Racism!... Global Warming!... (Whatever!)... AND IT'S ALL YOUR FAULT! I, personally, am tired of the hysteria. I am tired of the hyperbole. I am tired of being preached at by some arrogant, hypocritical media dufus (or worse yet, some arrogant, hypocritical Hollywood dufus) who has decided how I should think. I am also tired of being told it is all my fault, especially when I had nothing to do with whatever the world-ending alarming issue of the season may be. I'll take the risk of being vilified, but many cower under the threat of ridicule, and many are scared because they do not know what truly constitutes truth. The media owes us a giant mea culpa, but I don't expect one to be forthcoming.

None of this is good.

II. Maybe grace is absent because of our society's level of prosperity and self-sufficiency. Many people are going to take offense at my next comment, but the truth is the truth. This issue of prosperity and self-sufficiency applies even to people who are categorized as being in the poor segment of our society. I have seen dirt-poor people, and I know what that is all about. Those people have a tough life. In contrast though, a vast number of people are perceived to comprise part of the lower socio-economic class, yet they have tattoos (unnecessary and expensive), cell phones (unnecessary and expensive), professionally done manicures and fancy fingernail polish designs (unnecessary and expensive), and cars nicer than the ones I drive. Poverty, for them, may be a claim and a mindset, but it is not an actuality. Move up the ladder a notch to the middle class and look at the "essentials" that parents buy their teenage children. Move the level up another notch and look at the follies of the rich.

Many people may be legitimately scared, but we are truly an affluent society. Affluence makes us self-sufficient. That, in turn, means we don't need others. If others aren't needed, why be gracious?

III. The breakdown of the family structure, the massive number of divorces, and the redefinition of what constitutes a family certainly contributes to the problem. By eliminating the standards of a cohesive society we redefine what mannerisms and values are essential for society to function properly. A live-for-today, I-want-it-my- way society doesn't have room for grace.

Those may be the causes that manifest the symptoms. I believe that, if left unchecked, we are heading toward a condition of societal self-implosion. We cannot continue with these trends, and we cannot continue to ignore the root cause. The problems and manifestations we have grown accustom to will not go away by themselves.

The truth here is the need for society, individually and corporately, to stress the importance of grace and to practice it. We need to move from *"screw the other guy before he screws you"* to *"treat others as you want to be treated and give them the benefit of the doubt."*

This quest for grace is not a call to be stupid. We know there are self-serving people out there, so be on your guard against them. We know that, in all walks of life and in <u>every</u> socio-economic group, there are deceitful, nasty people, so (to the extent you are able) don't let them take advantage of you or prevail over you. Grace will help you contend with such people because it enables you to recognize their character and deal with them accordingly, while keeping your emotions separate from your actions. This may require a paradigm shift and will probably take practice, but learning to exercise grace will augment self-control.

Self-control has definite benefits. Discipline and self-control better enable you to be the person you want to be (that is, of course, unless you aspire to be a self-serving jerk, in which case you probably won't be reading this anyway). Every expression of self-control moves you in the direction of living a disciplined, grace-centered life.

Regarding people with whom you have to contend who may also debunk the notion of grace:

- Your actions may start to break down the walls they have built in their lives, the walls that make them, perhaps, nasty and contentious. (Let's expand this thought a bit. Your actions may start the process, but you may not get to witness the total transformation. That may take years.) It is appropriate to look at this as a long term process, because most people do not change their priorities and character overnight. The reality may be that the probability of any change at all is low.
- For those who choose to be nasty and contentious, the way you maintain control of the situation may only irritate them further, and they will want nothing to do with you. That makes you less vulnerable.

Either way, you benefit and grace wins.

Grace does not require me to be baselessly soft-hearted to the point of personal endangerment. I can be a most-gracious person, yet still look at a nasty, contentious, deceitful, self-serving person and say: If that is how they choose to live their life, they are putting themselves in harm's way. If a person chooses to put himself in harm's way, then he gets to experience the train wreck that defines his life. With no intention of sounding smug we can also acknowledge the fact that, by their choices, they brought it upon themselves. I can feel sorry for them, yet I know it is they who set their course in motion. Grace compels us to acknowledge emotions; prudence keeps us from letting emotions dictate actions. Grace and prudence are not mutually exclusive.

Moving on, let's go to the crux of the matter. We know there are good people out there too, people who are struggling to make it through the day. You may be one who is in that category. These folks should be our primary concern and focus. Grace enables us to believe in them, to help them as we are able, and to encourage them to persevere. By grace others may do the same for you and me.

"If you don't want trouble in your life, don't let trouble into your life" is a saying one of my friends often uses. That is a great phrase because it contains both outwardly directed and inwardly directed components. It literally means to make sure you hold close association only with quality people, and make sure you yourself are a quality person that others may want to hold close association with. Abiding in such a manner provides a buffer that enables you to deal with contentious people. Grace is easier to grant to others if you are not inundated with conflict as part of your normal daily existence.

Grace will never be universal in its extensions and applications. There will always be jerks to contend with. We just don't want them to be the dominant segment of society, nor do we want them to define the rules of conduct.

There is one other aspect of grace that fits well for me, though I realize others will reject the notion and anything associated with this second concept. It deals with another definition of grace provided by Webster: "the freely given, unmerited favor and love of God."

The two definitions cited work well together. Perhaps, in daily living, if we spend our time thinking about the latter we will be more inclined to do the former. It certainly will make for a better world.

Let me leave you with this thought:

Justice is getting what you deserved.

Mercy is NOT getting what you deserved.

Grace is getting what you DON'T deserve.[11]

---

[11] quote attributed to Cathleen Falsani

A Bite Out of the Apple

Musings follow, thoughts with questions that probably won't lead to answers. In this case answers aren't essential because they aren't the objective. Those are not what I'm striving for. Rather, the thoughts are what I want to concentrate on.

Initial thoughts lead to deeper thoughts and those may lead to conclusions. Conclusions lead to decisions; decisions lead to actions; actions lead to habits; habits lead to a lifestyle. The lifestyle I choose to live defines my legacy. I don't spend much time thinking about my legacy, however, since I would like it to be one of lifting up others, it's worth my time to stop and muse. In that regard here are my thoughts, the product of productive pondering:

- I want my wife to know she is much loved by me. That means I need to actively cultivate our relationship, share my thoughts with her, work together with her on common hopes and dreams, and in all things act in a manner that is in her best interest. Joy, peace, laughter, and affection need to be big parts of our relationship.

- I want to raise my children so they can enjoy thoughtful, happy, well balanced, successful lives. That means I need to parent them with discipline, structure, encouragement and positive reinforcement, and to provide all of those in balance in a peaceful, joyful (joy filled) home environment. I need to cultivate relationships with them, not to be their friend, but to be their father. Someone who will be their greatest advocate, comforter, and encourager; someone who seeks to guide them in their development; also someone who will lovingly take them to task when they screw up. Someone whom they genuinely enjoy being with because they know that I love them and their mother, and am totally committed to my family. I want them to be confident and to have strong senses of self-worth rooted in the knowledge that they are unique and significant parts of God's creation. I want them to show respect for others, and to cultivate gentle and humble spirits; to do good, and not be afraid to forcefully stand up against evil; to understand the meaning of integrity, and have it be an integral part of their character. For all those wants I need to lead by example. Laughter is equally important in these relationships. As I see it, a key mark of good parenting is for me to give my children greater opportunities to succeed than what I had. What that entails has nothing to do with wealth or material goods.

- I also want to help others so they experience a fullness of life that may be theirs. Much thought needs to go into just what that entails, but that is the reason for musing.

As the saying goes:
Sow a thought, reap an action.
Reap an action, establish a habit.
Establish a habit, define a lifestyle.
Define a lifestyle, set your destiny.
So it all starts in one's head.

As I sit and plunk away on a MacBook Pro computer I sometimes think of the creative genius who devised the machine. My thoughts trend to think of him more regarding his association with Pixar Studios though, rather than with Apple. Don't misunderstand, there is no maligning, nor anything negative intended toward either man or machine. The guy was amazing, and my laptop is a great computer. It is fast, reliable, functional, durable and well-constructed. I've had it for several years, and I put it to work daily. It has served me well and continues to do so.

I don't spend much time thinking about Apple though. The company makes great products yet I sometimes feel like there is a cult of Apple users and I don't want to join a cult. So instead, most often when I think of the afore-referenced man I think of Pixar. There good thoughts rest. In my mind Pixar connotes creativity and mirth, and I am a big fan of mirth.

I never met Steve Jobs, and he never met me. I suspect we are (were) both fine with that. I do wonder about his thought process though, the inner workings of his mind. Those are some of my musings.

Years ago I was told the name Apple came about because Mr. Jobs once worked at an apple orchard[12]. That explanation seemed weak to me. It would almost be like me naming my child Newspaper because I used to have a paper route, or Assembly Line, because I used to work in an auto factory. Those names were available, I guess, when my children were born, but I never thought to use them. In later years I heard it said that the logo held the true reason behind the Apple name.

By the Biblical account, the fall of man came about by Adam and Eve doing something they were told not to do, take a bite out of an apple God warned them not to eat. With the fall of man came the burdens of hard work. Mr. Jobs, so I was told, thought the burdens could be alleviated by technology. Since Steve and I never had a one-on-one conversation I can neither confirm nor deny that notion. It does provide a good point for musing though. Has technology alleviated mankind's burdens?

Delve into that consideration yourself. In a matter of minutes I can build support on either side of the question. In support thereof I need only reference anyone's experience typing a term paper in the pre-personal computer era. Cut & paste beats the dickens out of even IBM's best delete & edit function on a Selectric typewriter. Yet technology has brought to everyone's home a plethora of information, most of it relatively useless, that needs to be sorted through.

---

12 Walter Isaacson, in his biography of Steve Jobs, offers a different explanation regarding the origin of the Apple name.

Maybe a better question to ask is: Has technology made us more knowledgeable and self-reliant? Well, maybe. The abundance of information available through a few words typed into a search engine is overwhelming, yet we dump budget-busting amounts of money into our schools in pursuit of the latest technology, and standardized test scores - an assessment of knowledge - still don't approach levels commonplace elsewhere.

I suppose these musings could go on for a long time, but they don't lead to any meaningful thoughts.

I could compound the problem. Since the question posed pertains to technology and not just computers I could think on a broader scale and consider everything from the invention of the wheel to nano technology. Such efforts, though, will only compound my waste of time.

So I take a quantum leap and go in a different direction. Now my musings center on the question of what is it that gives people meaning in life? Is it levels of achievement in technological advancements, academic, or professional pursuits? Is it talent in sports, art, or music? Is it financial gains or accolades received? Is it relationships? In short, what is it that people make their god(s)?

What is it that people make to be their god? This is a musing worth spending time on because it reveals much about both human nature and people's identifiable defining characteristics. I find this interesting, because I find people-watching interesting.

Years ago I was looking forward to a scheduled trip to Las Vegas. This was in the era before we had Indian casinos on every street corner. I had never been to Vegas, but had heard many stories of the glitz and excitement, the fun of gambling, and the vast amounts of nonstop entertainment. I had funds designated for the slot machines and blackjack tables; like many other delusional nincompoops I hoped to win big, but I was also prepared to lose my gambling stash.

Anticipation lead to actuality, and actuality lead to awareness. I went to the casinos with $300 to spend, but after losing just $20 an epiphany hit. I realized:

1. I work hard to earn my money and I don't like wasting it.
2. Massive glitzy casinos don't get built because the house has a disadvantage.
3. I did not find fun that which I thought would be fun.

So I quit gambling and instead started watching other people. Then the fun began.

As I watched I concluded many of the folks I observed weren't having fun either. Some sat mindlessly pulling the lever of aptly named *one-arm bandits*; others sat pensively at various gaming tables; happy, gratuitous drunks staggered by (happy, I assume, until the hangover hit the next day), and others fought to maintain their vertical position on barstools. There wasn't the level of joy and festivity I anticipated, though. I don't think most of the people I watched were having fun, their body language certainly didn't suggest it. They were just out worshiping gods, and not seeing the folly of their actions. That last sentence sounds quite condescending and negative, but it's not meant to. It's just my observation of their reality.

Vegas-inclined people have their gods ("small 'g's" is how I think of them), other people have theirs. I'm not sure I'd say some are better and some are worse, though I may say some are more destructive than others.

Sometimes musings do lead to deeper thoughts and deeper thoughts lead to conclusions. After all my pondering one of my conclusions is that god status, the pursuit of those "small 'g's", whatever form it may take, won't get people where they really want to be. Now is probably a good time to leave those musings.

I read that Steve Jobs' last words were "Oh Wow, Oh Wow, Oh Wow."[13] I wonder what his mind saw as he took his last breath. I hope he now rests in peace, as millions wished upon hearing of his death.

---

[13] As cited in the eulogy for Steve Jobs given by Mona Simpson, his sister, on October 16, 2011. Reprinted in The New York Times, October 30, 2011

A Cold Reception to Manmade Global Warming

There are times where the disciplines required by one area of study translate over into another area of study. Such is the case with the current-day concern about manmade global warming. The ardent believers of that cause could learn and would benefit from one discipline associated with the proper rules of land surveying. Let me explain:

Located on Central Campus at the University of Michigan there stands a tall obelisk-type structure known as Burton Tower. It doesn't fit the true definition of an obelisk, but that reference helps create a mental image. Obelisks are square structures that taper from the base upward; on top is a pyramid-shaped cap. Burton Tower is a square structure that measures approximately 47 feet at the base. Unlike an obelisk the walls go straight up about 130 feet then inset a foot or so. Additional insets, larger than the first, occur at approximate heights of 174 feet and 189 feet above the ground. The walls top out somewhere around the 204 foot mark. A pyramid shaped roof then tapers up to a center point. The overall height of the tower is 212 feet. There is a large analog clock high up on each face.

A lightning rod is affixed to the peak of the tower's roof. I can only guess how big it is: a maximum diameter of 2 inches I suspect, and maybe 10 feet tall. I have spent more time looking at the lightning rod than any other single component of the structure. While engaged in that activity I always thought it courteous that the University built the tower underneath it just so I would have something to focus on. Most of the time I viewed the lightning rod from a distance of about 2 miles away while looking through instruments used for land surveying.

When surveying you set up a transit, or an even more precise instrument called a theodolite, over an identifiable location. That is known as your benchmark. You then sight on another identifiable location. That is known as your backsight. (The Burton Tower lightning rod served as my backsight.) The imaginary line that runs from your backsight to the benchmark creates the reference, the starting point, from which you proceed. A closed-loop survey requires that you return to your starting point, run a full circuit, to complete the process. Tolerances allowed for a proper survey are very tight: distance measurements need to "close" (sum up) to a matter of inches or fractions thereof; the sum of all angles need to close within a matter of minutes or seconds.[14]

One imperative of surveying is that you start by taking as long a backsight as possible. This is done for precision's sake. Long backsights promote overall accuracy. The converse of that statement, short backsights create the potential for errors, is also true. When pushing (extending) a survey line you want your backsight to be much greater in length than you intend to move forward. Not doing this increases the potential for skewing the line. If that happens the information you produce is not accurate. To attach numbers to this concept: You may use a 200 foot backsight to extend a line 50 feet; you would not want to use a 50 foot backsight to extend a line 200 feet.

Though I no longer survey I spent much time doing it early in my career. It is something I know well, and thoughts of it come to mind when I am involved in other activities. One day while musing I was thinking about the applicability of long backsights and realized it applies to other issues

---

[14] Similar to the time of day being broken into hours, minutes, and seconds, a circle has corresponding divisions. A full circle is comprised of 360 degrees; each degree can be further subdivided into 60 minutes; each minute can be further subdivided into 60 seconds. Thus, one second is 1/360th of one degree. Precision is required when surveying. Even minor deviances, when extended over long distances, will result in significant errors.

besides surveying. For example, think of it in terms of history or a historic event.

A long-known history provides a clear understanding of certain issues. You may get to see the beginning and have the opportunity to observe the nuances that occur as events unfold. Your observations may provide sufficient information to show a *cause and effect* relationship. Conversely, a short-known history does not provide the same breadth and depth of understanding. Observations and conclusions may be drawn, but the likelihood of accuracy diminishes significantly. Comprehension of causal relationships disappears completely.

It is on this notion that I find the idea of manmade global warming to be a troubling issue. I hear and read of authoritarian figures (and people who claim to be authorities) speak in an alarming tone about the damage wrought by man on the world's climate, yet I think, how do they know that? Their backsights aren't long enough to make such assessments and they do not possess the data needed to discern whether their observations are nuances or trends. Their postulates are based on assumptions and limited data, so their conclusions of cause and effect need to be challenged.

The reality is that we have about 200 years of reasonably accurate climatological data available for study, a generous estimate, and everything beyond that is based on assumptions made. On a time spectrum, when you compare what is definitively known to the age of the earth, that amount of time is rather insignificant. No one can take that limited amount of information and accurately project back to the beginning of time to say what was, then turn around and project forward to say what will be. 200 years' worth of data is insufficient to accurately predict the course of change through the earth's thousands, or millions, or billions of years of existence.

Now here is an interesting point to consider. At least I think it interesting, but some may say I am easily entertained. I ask, how old is the earth(?) and there are two broad answers. If you believe in cosmic-evolution the answer is "billions and billions" of years, ala Carl Sagen[15]. If you believe in the strict interpretation of the Bible regarding the creation story the answer is about six thousand years.[16] The purpose of this essay is not to argue the merits or weaknesses of either position. Here is the point to consider though: On the basis of applied reasoning, you are in a much better position to argue a global warming perspective as someone who believes in creation than you are if you believe in cosmic-evolution. 200 years' worth of known data relative to six thousand years total has to (heavy emphasis on has to) produce a better foundation for the assessment of analytical conditions than does 200 years' worth of known data relative to billions of years.[17] But here is the rub: Manmade global warming is more of a concern (for some a hysteria) of the cosmic-evolution-believing crowd than it is for the creation-believing crowd. I find this to be both ironic and quite humorous.

Some may attack this as a foolish, simplistic position on which to base an argument, but it should not be dismissed as such. Sometimes the understanding of profound scientific truths begin with a simple notion. For example, consider the chemical structure of benzine.

Scientists had known about benzine since the 15th century.[18] It wasn't until 1825 that the compound was first isolated by a man named Michael

---

[15] Carl Sagen was an astronomer, astrophysicist, author and television documentary host. Sagen is credited with claiming the universe is "billions and billions" of years old. He, however, insisted those were not his exact words, but rather a comedic misstatement of his words (which he found humorous) by television talk show host Johnny Carson. Sagen died in 1996.

[16] The age discussion for the two position (cosmic-evolution and creation) is presented simply as a cursory statement. To go into further detail would take us away from the topic of this essay. "Billions and billions of years", and "six thousand years" present the magnitudes of the two camps' positions regarding the age of the earth.

[17] 200 years of data relative to 6,000 years of earth's total existence equates to 3%. 200 years of data relative to two billion years (if that is the age of earth's existence) equates to 0.01%, one one-hundredth of one percent. That is a very small number.

[18] The name benzine wasn't used, but the compound was known and recognized because of its aroma.

Faraday, and it took another 40 years to determine its molecular make up. Credit is given to a German chemist named Friedrich August Kekule who published a scientific paper on the subject in 1865. Therein he postulated that benzine's chemical structure was a six-member ring of carbon atoms with alternating links of single and double bonds between the atoms. Kekule said the notion of this arrangement came to him while dreaming. A picture appeared in his mind of a snake eating its own tail.

As stated earlier, the point to be made with the benzine-related anecdote is that truth and discovery sometimes start with a simple notion.

Reluctance to buy-in to the popular notion of manmade global warming is not a flippant attitude on my part. Priorities of a higher order compel me to believe we should be good stewards of the earth: avail ourselves of but do not waste resources; maintain and promote a clean environment; live conservatively to minimize excessive consumption (and the need for landfills that are a byproduct of excessive consumption); and collectively, eat organic and non GMO food to the extent you are able, limit your intake of processed and prepackaged meals, make as many meals from scratch as you can. I'll stop short of worshiping the earth, though. Let's not make it a deity. That is both silly and a reflection of misplaced priorities.

I readily admit I tend to be jaded toward alarmist issues such as manmade global warming because I've seen the hysteria before, and true substance does not need hysteria. My first exposure to this was in the early 1970s. At that time the concern for control of environmental pollutants was just beginning. Many industries discharged untreated effluents into America's waterways. That was bad. Lake Erie, one of the five Great Lakes,[19] was an ecological nightmare due to the free flow of discharge from heavy industries located along the shores of Southeast Michigan and Northeast Ohio. The cause and concerns were valid - stop polluting - but the hysteria that went with it, "Lake Erie is a 'dead lake' and it will take a hundred

---

[19] It is estimated that the Great Lakes contain 20% of the world's fresh surface water.

years for it to recover" was a baseless claim. Within ten years the lake did a great job at cleaning itself up. All it needed was to stop the pollution. By the late 1970s sport fishing had returned to Lake Erie. Today the Western Basin of Lake Erie, an expansive, relatively shallow portion of the lake, is considered by some to have the best walleye fishing in the world. Revenue generated from sport fishing-related activities is a significant contributor to the local economy.

As I view the magnitude of nature as it goes through its gyrations I am inclined to believe that the earth is resilient, and man is puny. This foundational statement may be overlooked by many, and may even be rejected by most. Yet it should not be ignored.

My suspicion and negative reaction toward the hysteria of manmade global warming is also based on the character of some of its most ardent supporters. There is sometimes an accusation attached to this attitude where one is accused of shooting the messenger because they don't like the message. In this case that accusation cannot be applied. It is a matter of substance not matching style; of people who promote the cause not living lives consistent with their proclamations. It is prudent to cautiously decide in whom you will place your trust.

The challenge of character issue may be viewed by some as a superficial straw man argument, but it is not. (A straw man argument is one used to convolute a primary issue.) People who firmly believe in something act on their convictions; people who seek to benefit, monetarily or otherwise, are more inclined to say one thing but do another. Coupling hysteria and chicanery to the concerns of others can be highly profitable.

Genuine scientific discovery requires that you consider all facts, not just pick and choose those that support your position. It further demands that you pick apart the proofs of your position to affirm their validity. This becomes a challenge because most folks, me included, have limited ability to fully comprehend the salient points of the issue.

With such conditions our normal approach is to rely on experts to explain the intricacies of the matter to us. Here we are confronted by a twofold problem that limit those efforts:

1.   There is no consensus among the "experts". If you type the words "global warming" into a search engine you will access a data base that has about 50 million references attached. Typing the words "argument against global warming" produces about 38 million references. Good luck trying to make any sense of that.

2.   It is not well defined just what makes an expert an expert. Al Gore, former Vice President of the United States, received the acclaim of many for his movie <u>An Inconvenient Truth</u>. His background is not science though, so who made him an expert on the matter of global warming? Concerning Mr. Gore I have to question whether he has benefitted from the hysteria attached to this particular issue and is thus driven by ulterior motives. (In my opinion the short answer is yes.)[20]

In opposition stands an Englishman by the name and title of Christopher Monckton of Brenchley who produced a rebuttal titled <u>Thirty-five Inconvenient Truths - The Errors in Al Gore's Movie</u>. His rebuttal seems credible.

In reality though I have no firsthand knowledge of either man. To be dutiful in my quest I thus need to consider other sources to be well informed, and to have truth and reality as the foundation of my beliefs. Let's be prudent in whom we identify as being an expert.

Dr. Wallace Broecker is the man who coined the term global warming. His writings and research are interesting; his credentials vast and extensive; the regard for him in the scientific community, very high.

---

[20]   My opinion of Mr. Gore, resulting from his tenure as Vice President, is very low. With that stated prejudice others may challenge any comment I make regarding the man on the basis that I may be biased. My recommendation to those people is that they scribble out the words "may be" and insert the words "am, with cause."

Since he was the first to raise concerns regarding the issue of global warming his position cannot be dismissed as "group think" or following a trend. Yet as I look at the graphical presentation of his data[21] I have an immediate concern.

If you choose to look at the articles cited in the footnote you will see a graphical presentation of climate data relative to time. I do not know if the graph is Dr. Broecker's or someone else's, but here is my concern: As I looked at the XY graph associated with the analysis I noted the X-axis (time, segmented in years) shows small incremental spacing; the Y-axis (temperature, segmented in degrees Celsius) shows a narrow temperature range with large incremental spacing. The net effect of such a presentation is that it psychologically exaggerates the results of the analysis to the viewer. A one degree temperature change will look massive when presented in such a manner, yet it is still just a one degree temperature change. Big whoop.

So what do we choose to believe? In this earnest quest we (I) want the truth: true-truth, with fixed rigid standards, not a variable, conditional truth.

When in doubt go to the analytics, right? After all, numbers don't lie... or do they? Statisticians will tell you that the numbers don't lie, but they can be manipulated.

A frequently heard argument in support of manmade global warming is that analytical models have been built that provide all the evidence needed. Well, not really. Modeling is not an exact science.[22] Models based on people's behavior, their buying preferences, for example, can be relatively accurate because a key variable, human behavior, is well documented. On a macro scale this does not change. Variables used in the development of climatological models, however, are not as well documented nor are they

---

[21] reference http://thinkprogress.org/climate/ Walace Broeker's Remarkable 1975 Global Warming Prediction; The Warming World of Wally Broecker, 35 Years Later

[22] The process used by statisticians to project and assess future conditions based on currently known data is referred to as Time Series Modeling. It is a valuable tool used in many industries and academic areas of study.

fully understood. That makes these analyses susceptible to error.[23] The potential for error thus leads to a higher degree of uncertainty; the greater the degree of uncertainty, the less inclined one should be in treating the predictions as absolute truths. Yet those cautions have not been exercised.

Modeling is limited by another factor as well: Models cannot include random events. If they could the events would be scheduled, not random. Certain events significantly affect long term trends and developments. For example:

1. Mt. Pinatubo in the Philippines erupted in 1991. According to the U.S. Geological Survey (USGS) the blast sent 20 million tons of sulfur dioxide into the atmosphere which caused a three year drop in global temperatures of 1 degree (f). [24]
2. In 1980 the volcano sitting beneath Mt. St. Helen erupted, blowing 1,300 ft. of elevation off the top of the mountain and sending 50 million tons of ash into the atmosphere. It took seven months for the ash to settle out.
3. Even more cataclysmic, according to the USGS, a Mt. St. Helen eruption 3,600 years earlier was four times as large as the 1980 event.[25]

---

[23] Models associated with controversial subjects may be more prone to error. Preconceived prejudices may put undue emphasis on certain variables than what is later proved warranted, and these faults can easily carry over to other analyses when a group-think mentality comes into play. Models funded by third-party sources are particularly vulnerable. Statistical analyses are supposed to be conducted in a unbiased manner, but it is presumptuous to assume that is always the case. In defense of errors being inadvertently introduced, it is pertinent to note that real-world data is always messy, and facts are seldom readily apparent.

An underlying principle known as GIGO applies to this topic, of which every person needs to be highly mindful - GIGO: garbage in, garbage out. Every tool available should be used in the analysis process, yet it is also important to recognize their limitations.

[24] reference http://pubs.usgs.gov/gip.103/
[25] reference www.livescience.com/27553-mount-st-helen-eruption.html

Now let's complicate this further. Depending on how one views the creation of the world, randomness may define the rule of order. If cosmic-evolution is indeed a proper theory to apply, the world began as singularity[26] and there was no structure. Every development was random. Good luck building a model that will accurately describe that.

In need of consideration, too, there is a statistical term known as the *Cone of Confidence* that defines one limitation to the use of models. Picture a horizontal timeline with the left end labeled "Today", and the right end labeled "The Future". Now superimpose a cone over the line, with the apex positioned to the left. At any point along the line the distance between the top and bottom of the cone defines the range of possibilities for a given outcome on a particular issue. The greater the range of possibilities (the wider the cone), the less certain we are of any one specific outcome.

Let's play with this idea of "confidence" and use a "for instance" to see how it works. Let's predict the weather. Here goes:

It is December and I am in Michigan. For the last week it's been cold and snowy. What do I think:

tomorrow will be?	-	cold and snowy
the next day?	-	cold and snowy
next month?	-	probably cold; not sure about the snow
next March?	-	maybe cold, maybe snowy; I don't know
next December?	-	I don't know

Get the idea? It's easy to speculate about the near term and have a high degree of confidence that your assumptions will prove right. The further out you get though, the probability of any one specific condition drops.

---

[26] "Cosmic-evolution" pertains to the origin of the universe; (generically-termed) "evolution" pertains to the origin and development of life. They are two separate theories. For simplicity's sake, think of "singularity" this way: Singularity is to cosmic-evolution what primordial soup is to (generically-termed) evolution.

The further you are from the apex, the less the validity of any specific claims. Said a different way, to maintain the same level of confidence you will need to include more and more possible outcomes in the range of all possible outcomes.[27] One implication of applying the Cone of Confidence is that at some point you cross the line from proper statistical analysis to mere prognostications based on personal prejudices.

A genius of a man named Darrell Huff wrote a book titled <u>How to Lie Using Statistics</u>. Therein he stated that his intent wasn't to teach folks how to lie, rather he wanted to make people aware of the ploys others may use. One of the best lines of the book reads: "Many people use statistics like a drunk uses a lamp post: for support, not illumination." My concern is that analytical models used to prove manmade global warming are culpable of Mr. Huff's admonition.

Regarding the issue of manmade global warming I do find the postulates that people present in support of their position to be interesting. Sound scientific methodology and reasoning may have governed the development of their studies. I appreciate their work for two reasons:

1. Even though initial premises are usually flawed, all discovery has to have a starting point.
2. Being someone who believes in God, I view science as his way of revealing to us how he created everything. Johannes Kepler,[28] a 17th century mathematician, termed science as "thinking God's thoughts after Him."

---

[27] Statisticians do not consider a single event or outcome. They look at a term called "confidence intervals" which refers to the likelihood that something will fall within a given range of parameters. As information becomes more obscure you need to consider more possible outcomes to maintain the same level of confidence. As you consider more outcomes the range increases in size. Those discussions go way deeper than anything intended by this essay.

[28] Kepler is best known for his laws of planetary motion. His works provided the foundation for Isaac Newton's theory of universal gravitation. You can read about Kepler in Wikipedia. What is written therein is interesting.

I can respect, yet still refute, the findings of those who believe in manmade global warming because I also know this fact: If initial assumptions are flawed or baseless, then everything that follows is flawed and baseless. That is one of the fundamental laws of mathematics. Baselessness comes with presumptions and with sweeping assumptions made concerning cause and effect.

At this point any devotee of the cause may argue that I have not disproved anything. Relative to a future time spectrum that could be a true statement. (Just because something hasn't yet happened does not mean that it won't happen would be the basis of their argument.) But who can legitimately argue the future unknowns? On a stronger basis, my refute would be that they cannot defend against the errors of their claim. That applies to the premise as a whole, and in their failure to draw the distinctions between a nuance and a trend. The importance of the afore-stated relationship (200 years of available climatological data relative to the age of the earth) is self-evident.

As it pertains to global warming, here is my bottom line: Those who believe that global warming is caused by man do not have backsights long enough to support their postulates. That is a rule I learned from surveying. The conclusions expressed, overly pontificated I may add, are not based in applied science. What we have are conclusions drawn from applied supposition.

So what is the purpose of this essay? Perhaps there are a couple lessons contained herein:

- A willingness to question authority is one lesson to keep in mind. Determine for yourself what authority you will place your trust in. This is important because some who present themselves with such credentials may not be what they say they are. They may have all the accoutrements and accolades - position, power, status, wealth, beauty, eloquence - but those are just image issues. Those attributes do not define the caliber of a person, nor the validity of their position.

- Be mindful of people with hidden agendas is a second lesson. People will say and purport issues and positions as truth. There is value in asking: "Is it truly so?"
- Validate what is being said is always an important lesson to keep in mind. Where is the proof; where is the track record; where is the support? In this regard it is always good to ask yourself: "How does (a particular issue) fit with other things I know to be true?" That is always a good question to ask. A healthy dose of skepticism now may save you from much aggravation and embarrassment later.
- A friend of mine from graduate school (Mike, who now lives in Oklahoma) once told me a rule that is worth remembering. Whenever Mike hears someone speak on a potentially contentious subject, he listens, but also pictures the person having five letters tattooed across their forehead: W I I F H; What's In It For Him?
- Don't be afraid to stand against the crowd. Just because something is popular or a common perception, that does not make it right or true. Standing alone won't necessarily put you in a contentious position, though it may. What is more important, it simply means you will not allow yourself to be subject to group think and you place a high value on the discovery of truth. I admire those qualities in people. If you later determine your position is wrong you are free to change and move on. That is allowed. The reality in the true application of scientific methodology is that you seldom get things right the first time, and that is OK. Keep working at it; enlightenment may come.

I tend to like the validations of properly applied scientific methods. Like I said earlier, science is man discovering how God created everything. Not everything claimed to be applied scientific methodology is though, so validate.

There is one last point to mention regarding the argument of manmade global warming. Once we get through all the discussions of what is and what isn't; of what is evidence and what is supposition; of what is truth and what is conjecture, I have one other thought about manmade global warming. I think it is a secondary issue and a secondary argument, not the crux.

The primary issue is what people believe regarding how the earth was made:

- Cosmic-evolution, something from nothing, order from chaos, every event is random; or
- The creation of a creator, intelligent design, the progression of planned structure, God.

Where people position themselves on this topic serves as a strong predictor for what their position will be on secondary issues such as the topic of manmade global warming and the concerns associated therewith.

Let's face reality. For all the antagonisms that exist regarding global warming this is what every argument eventually boils down to: The respective core belief of each side of the argument is what guides the thought process on everything else.

Here is a point that is important to consider and remember, both as it pertains to global warming and to others issues where there may be contention: When only secondary issues are discussed and the primary issue is ignored, there is little chance of anyone being persuaded from their way of thinking. Regarding this matter of global warming though, let's be truthful about this too: It is the man-caused believing crowd that is the more caustic of the two in their condescension and expressed opinion of the other side. Sadly, you even see powerful people such as the current President of the United States - someone with absolutely no scientific background - devolve into the thoughtless and inflammatory practice of name-calling. This accomplishes nothing. Enlightenment should be the reason for, and purpose of, debate and discussion. Not everyone has that objective.

I find one element of our human condition to be somewhat humorous: We know very little of the world around us and the universe of which we are a part, yet we talk and act as though we know so much. I once read that the person in charge of the U.S. Patent Office in the late 1800s recommended the department be abolished because he believed everything that could be invented had already been invented, an obvious misperception of reality. I kinda think people who get caught up in the hysteria of manmade global warming have succumbed to a similar misperception. We think we know so much, but in reality we know very little.

~ Epilogue ~

Thirteen months have passed since I wrote this essay, and the book is now in its final stage of editing prior to publication. Over that period of time an interesting shift occurred in the way this topic is presented. *Manmade Global Warming* is no longer used as the topical title. It is now referred to as *Manmade Climate Change*. Observant people have cause to ask: Why the new vernacular, the shift in subject matter? Prudent people already know the answer to that question.

This accusation of an assumed manmade calamity now has its third label. When research regarding man's influence on the carbon cycle first became a popular topic of conversation the concern was that increased levels of carbon dioxide (CO_2) would lead to Global Cooling (label #1). Once it became apparent that the evidence didn't support the prognostications the focus shifted to Global Warming (label #2). Once again evidence apparently does not support the prognostications so label #3, Global Climate Change, is now used.

Second only to the nasty arrogance and vindictiveness of some people, what complicates discovery regarding global climate change is that this topic has become more a political issue than it is a scientific issue.

The reality is that much discovery still needs to take place. Generally-assumed-to-be-true principles may not be so in actuality. For instance, consider the assumption that CO_2 is a primary destructive greenhouse gas.

People more knowledgeable than I claim it is not the destructive agent it has been made out to be.[29]

We do know the prognostications regarding manmade global warming have not occurred, but we do not know whether the evidence of global climate change is a nuance or a trend. Our backsights are not long enough to definitively state one or the other. For true knowledge and understanding to advance, this is what's important: keep discussions and research open and ongoing - that is where discovery comes from - but stop the name calling and belittling of people who do not agree with a set position.

---

[29] Reference PlantsNeedCO2.org. For additional information on this topic type "climate change debunked" into a search engine.

Choices This Side of the Grave

Here is something I read recently:

"In the beginning God created the heavens and the earth. The earth was without form, and void, and darkness was on the face of the deep. And the Spirit of God was hovering over the face of the waters.

Then God said, 'Let there be light'; and there was light. And God saw the light, that it was good, and God divided the light from the darkness. God called the light Day, and the darkness He called Night. So the evening and the morning were the first day."

In terms of the words used, the sentences written above are not complex. Yet I cannot fully tell you what they mean. I understand the part about God creating the heavens and the earth, but the part about God's Spirit hovering is where explanation escapes me. Conceptually I grasp the word picture; perhaps it's a way of saying that God has forever been in existence. Don't take my word on that, though. If there is a deeper meaning I don't want you to miss it.

The uncertainty doesn't stop there, it gets worse. If you follow the story the next section reads:

"Then God said, 'Let there be a firmament in the midst of the waters, and let it divide the waters from the waters.' Thus God made the firmament, and divided the waters which were under the firmament from the waters which were above the firmament; and it was so. And God called the firmament Heaven. So the evening and the morning were the second day."

Those two passages comprise verses 1- 8 of the first chapter of Genesis, the first book of the Bible. They are the beginning of the Bible's explanation of how all things were created, the Creation story. It continues through a page-worth of additional information. In truncated form (shown below) what we read next is:

Then God set the form of the Earth, with dry land and seas, and he brought forth foliage and fauna according to their kind.

Then God established the seasons, and made the sun, moon and stars.

Then God made the creatures of the sea according to their kind and the winged birds of the air according to its kind.

Through each event "God saw that it was good"; and "So the evening and the morning" identifies days three, four, and five.

Then God made the living creatures of the land, each according to its kind. Then God said, "Let Us make man in Our image, according to Our likeness..." And God made man and woman.

"Then God saw everything that He had made, and indeed it was very good. So the evening and the morning were the sixth day."[30]

And on the seventh day God ended his work and he rested.

Welp, plenty of opportunity for confusion and uncertainty there; plenty for an inquisitive mind to sort through(!)

I can't explain all of what I read in the Bible, but I do not reject it. It's kinda like what Mark Twain said: "It's not the parts of the Bible I don't understand that cause me trouble, it's the parts I do understand that cause me trouble." (I think he meant something other than what I do, though.) By my reasoning, if you are the God of all creation then you can

---

[30] Cited quotes may be found in Genesis 1: 1-30; the last quote is Genesis 1:31

pretty-much do whatever you want; and since God is, he can. I accept that. It is not important that I try to explain God's every move. He does not need me to be his apologist. I admit my prejudices toward the Creation account, but at this time will forego the assessments and justification. They exist, but that is not the crux of this essay. My greater concern is for others who struggle with uncertainty.

Lack of understanding can drive people away, not only from the Bible, but also from any belief in God. Rather than dig into the unknowns and pursue a quest of discovery, they reject all in its entirety. That is a choice they make. For people who reject the Bible and those who don't believe in God, I would ask if it is easier to believe in evolution? You'll have to read through my humor and my bias, but this is how I sum that theory up:

In the beginning there was nothing but randomness and chaos
and then something happened but there was still no life
But there was energy and there was primordial soup
And then the energy and the primordial soup hooked up
and then out of the primordial soup emerged
a single-cell living organism
Then over millions; no, I mean hundreds of
millions; no, I mean billions of years
every living thing evolved until the way things are today
And we have elaborate, well organized theories to prove it
right down to the orientation of amino acids
which are the building blocks of life
Amino acids can have left-hand orientation and right-hand orientation,
similar to the way our bodies have a left hand and a right hand
They are the same, but mirror images of one another
And to sustain life some amino acids must have a left-hand orientation
and others must have a right-hand orientation
(and by the way, one cannot be substituted for the other)
And through evolution
- a systematic but unstructured weeding-out process -
an incredibly complex and organized system of
properly oriented molecules developed

so the amino acids can do the things they have to do
in order for us to have life
And we have DNA which is the recipe for every living thing
Every living thing has its own unique DNA
And keeping in mind the premise that all life
originated from a single-cell organism
the implication is that many and every DNA recipe evolved from one
but each is now unique
But don't ask me how the recipe evolved
Or who had the original recipe in the first place
Isn't evolution grand!

By my thought process a belief in evolution, the idea that what works survives and thrives, and what doesn't work falls away, contains a circular argument. In order to affirm and prove evolution you need to present that which did not survive, but you cannot present it, because it no longer exists, it didn't survive. Therefore you just have to believe.[31]

In support of my beliefs I would cite a quote attributed to Blaise Pascal, a 17th century mathematician and philosopher: "The heart has its reasons which reason cannot know." In rejection of that which I do not believe I would cite a quote attributed to Voltaire, an 18th century philosopher: "Common sense is not so common." But I readily admit my prejudices.

Now here is a funny point to consider: People with beliefs other than mine can use those same quotes against me. After all, their beliefs may be just as heart-felt as mine, and they may wonder if I am void of common sense.

This brings us to a distinction that is important to realize: We treat science and Christianity as though they stand in opposition to each other, yet that is not true. Conflict does exist between Christian beliefs and

---

[31] There exists a school of thought based on the premise that, perhaps, evolution is the mechanism through which God created everything. I do not ascribe to that belief - it does not mesh well with my understanding of the statements cited earlier, "each according to its/their kind" - yet there are many exceedingly-smart, accomplished scientists who hold solid Christian beliefs, for whom there is no conflict.

something referred to as "scientism", a belief that only empirically-based, verifiable knowledge is valid (which thus makes scientism an object of worship, and a strict religious order in and of itself). This is the antagonism that is generally, though incorrectly, thought of as existing on a larger scale. (... good for the media, bad for truth.) When the extremes of either side define the rules of engagement, conflict will ensue. In contrast, it is important for people to understand that there are many devote Christians actively involved in scientific pursuits and discovery. It has been that way through all of history, and it is on-going today.[32] An admonition of a guy named John Ortberg is to follow truth <u>ruthlessly</u>. Holding fast to well-founded Biblical beliefs and embracing the knowledge that comes through true scientific discovery are not mutually-exclusive endeavors.

With the foundation that has just been laid let's now move to the crux of this essay. I can wrap this up fast, but I hope thoughts will linger that will cause you to do a bit of introspection. Choose for yourself, determine for yourself, what it is that you believe. Know what you believe, and understand why you believe.

What I ask is that you not be complicit in intellectual complacency. By definition, intellectual complacency is the process by which someone makes decisions that require serious and in-depth thought, without first taking time to work through the in-depth thought process. This is sometimes described as having thoughts a mile wide and an inch deep. That is a good thing to avoid yet, to some extent, we all may be guilty of it. It may, perhaps, be a process we have to discipline ourselves away from. Some people mature away from it; others never do.

---

[32] If you find the pursuit of discovery interesting, go to this link: <u>http://biologos.org/blog/john-ortberg-sermon-does-science-disprove-faith</u>. The lecture will take about 40 minutes to listen to, or you can read a printed transcript. Either way, it is time well spent. This will also get you to the homepage for the BioLogos Foundation website (biologos.org). Therein can be found the organization's statement titled <u>What We Believe</u>. What is written therein should not offend the senses of anyone who firmly embraces Christian doctrine as their core beliefs, even though they may not concur with every point written. Certain issues will always be open to debate and discussion.

With that notion in mind, please consider the fact that *Creation v. Evolution* is not a stand-alone debate. At its core there is a deeper consideration, a more in-depth question waiting to be answered. The real issue is contained in the question:

> *Where do you place your hope, in the sufficiency of God,*
> *or in the sufficiency of man's intellect (self)?*

Each and everyone of us, individually, gets to make that decision; each of us gets to choose. A well-founded answer has more to do with one applying their full intellectual capacity than it does with one not applying their full intellectual capacity.

There are many choices we get to make this side of the grave that define what we believe and how we behave, the determinants of our individual character. This issue of sufficiency is an important one to consider. It significantly affects the way you think and act, and what you assign as priorities for your life.

Follow the Money Trail - Keeping an Eye on ~~Personal Finances~~ Life

A good number of years ago, 25 or more, I read a book written by a fellow who had made a lot of money. I don't remember the guy's name nor the title of his book. I do recall he made his fortune in real estate, but I don't recall most of what he wrote. The book read well though and I found it interesting. I was at the onset of my career and there was one topic the author stressed that stuck with me. Though at the time of the book's writing the author had established his success, he wrote in detail about his failures. That may be part of what made the book read so well.

Listening to people brag about their success and pat themselves on the back gets dull fast. I always wonder how much embellishment of the truth goes into those stories. When people talk about their failures though, they are not out to impress, and they are typically forthright with their words. They don't need affirmation and they're not looking to achieve god status. Most often their motivation is to say: "Here is something I did that was dumb. Avoid it."

A comment worth remembering pertained to mistakes the guy made along the way: poor planning, bad decision making, putting trust in people who proved themselves untrustworthy. He estimated the cost of those mistakes to be about $200,000. That got my attention and I wondered how he could write about it in such a cavalier manner. The obvious answer was that he was writing about it after the fact and he had already worked through whatever emotions he felt at the time. His paradigm was different from mine, but I hoped never to have a similar story to tell. That didn't happen.

In relative terms with values adjusted for inflation I'm not sure how my numbers compare. I knew the magnitude but I never wanted to know the exact amount. That was moot and painful to boot. (ha ha, a rhyme). Enough time has passed and I've purged many of the details from my mind. The loss came about for the same reasons though: poor planning, bad decision making, and putting trust in people who proved themselves to be untrustworthy. Those three factors work in concert like the necessary components for fire: fuel, oxygen, and heat. Combine all three, and something gets burned.

My loss didn't come all at once, rather I got to experience the "death by a thousand cuts" method of torture as events unfolded over the course of eighteen months. Most of the details aren't worth mentioning here, but I did scrutinize and replay the events to the point of ad nauseam because I had to learn from my mistakes. The biggest lesson learned, the largest revelation, was that I thought I was doing things right but I ignored warning signs along the way. Had I paid attention and given proper credence to those warning signs I could have cut my loss in half. I may not have entered into the wealth-destroying deal at all.

For emphasis I am going to change the wording of a sentence I just wrote. This is where truth leaks out: **I deluded myself into believing I was doing things right <u>by</u> ignoring warning signs along the way.** I wanted to believe in the "goodness" of what I was doing and believe likewise in my associates, but to do so I had to ignore several issues that were staring me in the face (growling) and screaming in my ears.

Maybe this a good time to comment on several lessons learned:

1. **Poor planning makes you vulnerable**. If you do not have a well-developed plan you will not have good landmarks to assess if things are progressing as you want them to. In financial matters, and in personal matters, you need to know where you stand and in what direction things are trending. **Fail to plan, plan to fail** is a good adage to keep in mind.

2. Another point to be mindful of is the complexity of your plan. A good rule to remember is: **The more complex your plans, the greater the likelihood that you will fail.** If you need many factors to come together, or if your plans require long-term commitments, you must have a means to evaluate progress at any moment, and be able to limit your exposure (financial obligations, personal risk) until every limiting factor is behind you. There is an acronym that applies to military matters and business planning: KISS - Keep It Simple, Stupid.

3. Bad decision making clouds the issues. Note, the emphasis here is on the process (decision making) more so than it is on the outcome. **If you put desires and aspirations ahead of prudence, you will fail.** This holds true even if your aspirations are admirable and your goals notable and worthy of respect. This point should serve as an admonition for you to be mindful of your emotions. Humans are emotional by design, and emotions can be deceiving. Be particularly cautious with this issue. The more noteworthy your goals, the more susceptible you may be to bad decision making.

4. Be mindful and conservative, and exercise extreme caution when you decide in whom you will put your trust. This is a critical point to keep in mind when dealing with financial matters, life issues, and decisions that may affect public perceptions of your character and integrity. (Stop and reread the last two sentences again, slowly. While you are at it, reread point # 3, too.) Do not allow emotions to influence these decisions. My business associates masqueraded as upstanding members of the community, but casual comments made during business meetings revealed character traits and core values not observed by most. Here is a very important point to remember: **When what you see doesn't mesh with what you hear, get leery fast.**

I know all those things, and I knew them then, but I continued anyway, with hope beyond hope. Lessons learned.

Most people will not put themselves in the situation I did, yet they readily make life-defining decisions that make them much more vulnerable.

Though difficult, humbling, and challenging, recovery from financial disasters can happen regardless of how brutal the disaster may be. Poor decisions made on life-related issues, however, will literally last a lifetime. Worse still, the results of our poor decision making may affect the opportunities of future generations.

That brings us to the crux of the matter: poor decisions that are now affecting future generations. We have walked a long path that is taking our society in a direction we really do not/should not want to go, but we mindlessly proceed, and foolishly affirm that all is well.

I may take a lot of heat for the words to follow, so with no apologies let me first throw out a few disclaimers. These set the stage. Continue at your own risk, because things are going to get ugly.

- Some who read the words to follow may be offended. My intent is neither to criticize nor offend. It is to say look where we have come from and look where we are today. Then use common sense to assess the change and you should conclude, as I have, that the change is not good. Then consider where we are heading. Then use common sense to assess the anticipated change and you should conclude, as I have, that the anticipated change is not good.
- Some people may view things differently, and I am fine with that. To this group I say please tell me your assessment of the situation and your solution for the problems we face. I value education and hope someone can prove my premises wrong. If proven wrong I will readily and joyfully admit it. If, however, the basis of your argument is "I want what I want regardless of the consequences" please don't waste my time.
- Having read what follows some may call me a puritanical fool. Maybe I am, and you are free to think of me whatever you want; but I am also right, and truth has to leak out. (By the way also, the inference of the accusation is not necessarily an accurate use of the adjective.)

- Some may say what I claim to be the truth is merely my opinion. I'll respond by acknowledging it is my opinion and it is also the truth as supported by all the evidence around us.
- Some may vilify me just because they don't like what I write. Many find it easier to malign the other guy than face up to the fact that they are wrong. I am OK with that because a quote of Winston Churchill (the guy who gave Great Britain the will to fight against the devastating onslaughts of Nazi Germany during World War II) comes to mind.

Never one to avoid confrontation, Churchill was once asked: "Doesn't it bother you what (these people) say about you?" Churchill's reply was: "If I thought they knew what they were talking about, or cared for their opinion, it would. But I don't, and I don't, so it doesn't." Ditto, me.

So if anyone wants to rant against me, that is OK. Rants and diatribes directed against me won't fix the problems we have created, though.

Here is the truth: Most folks who comprise today's younger generations are vulnerable in ways they don't realize. And it is the folly of older generations, by disregarding the evidence brought about by the decline in societal standards, that has created this condition. I'll leave it to you to define the generational split between younger and older; by my assessment I fall firmly in the latter group.

To put things in their proper perspective lets saunter back to 1973. I don't know why I recall so well one conversation that occurred, yet I can picture the event to this day. I sat with a couple guys in some college class and we had a group project to complete. These guys were classmates of mine but not my buddies, so once the semester was over our relationship ended.

During a break in one work session a couple guys started talking about their sexual escapades from the weekend before. Never have I understood why that happens, nor do I understand the motivation behind it. Why anyone would think I want to hear about their exploits is beyond me. If they are out to impress, they fail.

Whenever some fool starts down that road two thoughts typically come to my mind:

1. Guys lie and guys exaggerate. My general suspicion is that most of what they are about to say is concocted, unverifiable, and not true. I think of them as nothing more than insecure idiots with misplaced priorities and I have no interest in hearing about their outrageous fantasies.

2. I wonder if the woman of whom the jerk speaks knows that what she does in private and confidence does not stay private. Moreover, I wonder if women know that guys lie, exaggerate and embellish the truth at the expense of women's characters. Secrets that should remain secret are not kept so, and wherever lines do get drawn these loudmouth-type guys will claim to have crossed them.

I have no interest in listening to such boasting and typically tune out the conversation. This time though I remember looking at the two loudmouths and thinking: You guys are liars; absolute, abject, unadulterated liars, and you make yourself out to be fools. The deeper part of my thought was: Those guys have missed out on the then-unfolding sexual revolution they assumed everyone else was a part of, so they had to say things they thought would make them fit in. How foolish, how insecure, and how destructive.

The lies and desires of those clowns, as well as those of most of the Western world, have now fomented for more than forty years. If you consider the seeds of change that germinated in the 1960s we are at the fifty year mark. The national awaking of sexual liberation so many lusted to be a part of has, in actuality, wreaked havoc on our nation. Societally we pat ourselves on the back and say it's all good, and we commend ourselves for not being hypocritical like earlier generations that would be less inclined to broadcast things done in confidence and in secret. That, in itself, is grossly hypocritical. We learned lessons of lies, hurts, and betrayals, but sequester them, because they don't conform to what we want to claim as truth. All the while we deny the realities that are before us.

Here are the products of these wonderful (new) mores that so many give nodding ascent to:

- Divorce rates have now crossed the 50% mark (52% was the latest statistic I heard). With each divorce the hope of stability that comes through an edifying family structure goes out the window. Rather than working through problems to rekindle a once desirous relationship, individuals bail and leave generational carnage in their wake. Very few, I believe, are the number of relationships where problems don't develop at some point. Most of those problems, however, can be reconciled. A core reason for the shallowness of many fractured relationships is that they were not first given the opportunity to develop deep roots. The power and drive for sexual intimacies were allowed to supersede other factors needed to lay a foundation of respect and trust.

- An alternative to marriage is to first live together to "make sure you are compatible." This arrangement is far from being revolutionary. Folks have been doing that for a long time, though it is now more readily accepted than it once was. It is, however, a deceitful notion that makes you more susceptible to loss and failure than you can imagine when you are considering this option. That is the reason it was once societally frowned upon - a concern about what was being ignored, the potential for others' losses and failures. When surging hormones are active nothing else seems to matter. Here is the fallacy no one talks about today though: Surging hormones won't surge through the 30, 40, 60 or however many years remaining in your life. If that is all you are now building a relationship on, you will in time have a relationship built on nothing.

In this environment the appeal of sex does have a tendency to hamper the development of a relationship that will endure. You do not know what you miss out on when you make this choice. It is akin to reducing the alphabet to abc-xyz. There is a lot in the middle of relational growth that is missed, yet you don't realize that, because you're not aware it even exists. The relational growth process has had the middle chopped out of it.

Note as well that these relationships, by their very nature, are void of long term commitment. In every capacity the exchange between parties only address and satisfy short term needs and conditions. With very few exceptions, these relationships do not last.

My admonition to folks who think I am a fool for writing this is to get ready to live a life of hurt and poverty. You may be vulnerable in ways you cannot imagine. You are looking at today, and not giving consideration to the future ramifications of what today's actions may bring. So my admonition is not driven by condescension, it is offered out of concern.

Pay attention please: I have never heard anyone say that living through the process of a fractured relationship is a fun experience. There is always hurt and a sense of loss, with the possible exception of someone who is themselves a self-absorbed, shallow jerk. Divorce, which includes the termination of cohabitating, commingling-of-assets relationships, typically devastates at least one party, and it always destroys wealth.

Women are particularly vulnerable. For years sociological studies have pointed to the fact that the number one cause of poverty among women is the birth of children out of wedlock. So women, please may I politely implore you to run from the guy who says the two of you should move in together. Once you go in that direction it is very difficult to undo the consequences of what will most likely prove to be a very big mistake.

Guys, likewise, be leery of the woman who says you should live together. You may be nothing more than a temporary accommodation. Any desire you have to develop a long term, mutually edifying relationship will be challenged by that arrangement. If through the course of that relationship you give life to a child you will have an eighteen year obligation of financial support regardless of whether the relationship survives or not. The courts, if you attempt to avoid that obligation, will not be empathetic to your plight. Your financial well-being means nothing to them when held in balance against a child's well-being. You will work only to give away most of what you earn. If you are willing to man-up, you will have to admit that you brought it upon yourself.

As a footnote, the way a man and woman, or young man and young woman, find out if they are compatible is for them to mutually decide they want to be compatible. Statistically speaking the greatest potential for success in establishing long-term compatibility is if this happens long before sex enters the picture. You need to get to know each other's interests and personalities; each other's core beliefs and character; the deep thoughts that are not revealed to others (by another name, intimacy at a soulful level); the building of a relationship. That takes time and effort.

If those efforts build on a foundation that goes beyond the initial mutual interest and attraction you then choose to be compatible: Choose each day to seek what is best for the other person; choose to make your interests secondary to the other's interests; choose to have a propriety in your relationship where you never have to regret your actions individually or collectively, or cause loss, humiliation, or sorrow to your partner; choose that you will hold to these commitments every day for the rest of your life, and affirm them every day for the rest of your life (and forgive one another when mistakes are made, which will happen). Make those commitments, with each intentionally submitting to the other out of love and mutual respect, and you will be compatible through the rest of your lives. This is what provides the foundation for you and that person to whom you are now attracted to experience that which so few get to enjoy: A marriage that will last a lifetime.

A final comment, this is where truth leaks out: sex, an active intimate physical relationship prior to and outside the bounds of marriage greatly diminishes the likelihood that that lifelong commitment will last a lifetime. It is not just me making that statement and it did not originate with me. It is the evidence of the statistical analysis of marriage and divorce, as conducted by numerous sociological studies that all draw the same conclusion.

When you minimize the value of a traditional family structure,

- one with a man and woman, husband and wife committed to each other;
- where there exists the added common bond of a desire to create a positive, cohesive family in which children can grow, learn from observing their parents, know that people care about them, and that they have value,

you compromise the foundation that enables children to mature into stable adulthood, and you fracture the structure of a stable society. The result is that you create the segue for a baseless generation. Why do you think there is so much gang participation, teenage suicide, drug use (and other methods of escaping reality), and kids killing kids? The root cause lies in our innate desires for belongingness, stability, family, and purposeful meaning. When you remove structure; when you remove the value of stable, loving relationships; when you remove a belief in and an understanding of God; when you reduce the worth of a child to nothing more than the biological byproduct of a biological father having an intimate relationship with a biological mother, all sense of self-worth and value of human life goes by the wayside.

By this same mindset, whereby we reduce the value of human life and dignity to nothingness, men callously tell their pregnant girlfriend to get an abortion because "a child would be inconvenient" for the relationship; and women get them, even partial birth late term, telling herself it is just a "nonviable mass". Though legal and societally acceptable, I am told no woman who has undergone the procedure ever forgets the date. Conscience is convicting.

That last statement may be harsh, but it is neither meant to vilify and condemn, nor to condescend. The reality of the situation is that there is a very sad tragedy played out - over and over again, repeatedly - but rather than face up to the truth, the pro-abortion contingency of our society masks it. The reality of every abortion is that a child is dead, or would you prefer to say "made nonviable"(?) The reality of many abortions is that there is now a mother hurt and wounded, sometimes with a depth of guilt that cannot be assuaged. My heart earnestly mourns for those women.

They bought into a lie, perhaps with reservation or against their better judgment, perhaps unknowingly or without full information, but still a lie. These women are now casualties who need restorative help to enable them to recover and move on, help that is seldom there.

There are also women who die with their feet in the stirrups. Do not for a moment believe the lies that are so often implied. Babies are not the only ones to die in "safe, legal" abortion clinics.

All this from a society that makes the claim of protecting women and children. I don't get it. Our delusions and depths of denial are seemingly boundless.

There is one final point that needs to be made. If you have not yet read the essay titled <u>Table Manners</u> please do so as soon as you are able and pay particular attention to the story regarding Bear Bryant. That story contains an example of what happens when you have in place the benefits of an intact family structure: the multigenerational influence of a patriarch on a younger generation, and the apparent respect the younger generation has for the wisdom and guidance from the older.

As an extension of the "one final point" listed above, please be mindful of this, too: Children who come from fractured homes or from poorly-defined family structures do not have the same opportunities to succeed as do children who come from nurturing, intact family units; and the challenges they face are much greater. They do not have the same level of nurturing support, direction, and affirmations as did the young man in Bear Bryant's story.

On that premise here is something you now know: The next time you hear someone whining about social inequality, income inequality, educational-opportunity inequality, or whatever the (fill-in-the-blank)-inequality of the day may be, think to yourself, "I know better." The greatest limiting factor, that which supersedes all the above, is *family inequality*. By and large, family inequality is the primary reason why those others are prevalent. And for the most-part, on a per-family basis, family inequality is brought about through the personal choices of a couple of individuals, not because of the other ills of our society.

Here is what the last 3,965 words you just read boil down to: When you abandon the traditional family structure - one marriage that endures, where patriarchs and matriarchs are able to provide guidance to subsequent generations, and replace it with anything else - going in and out of the marriage/divorce cycle, cohabitation and children growing up without the benefit of an intact family structure, homosexual relationships - you lose the benefit of a nurturing, stable environment, one where children learn from older generations and are better prepared to grow into adulthood.

Putting it bluntly, if you ascribe to any of the alternatives just mentioned you condemn the generations that follow. You make their struggle much greater, and their opportunity for getting to enjoy a higher standard of living significantly less.

So for anyone who ascribes to the standards to which our society has devolved, the lessons I learned are now the same ones I implore you to consider. I earnestly ask this out of concern, for you are vulnerable to hurt, sorrow, and loss. If you continue down a poorly-chosen path you may not have the opportunity to recover.

- **When what you see and hear doesn't mesh with what you know to be true and right, get leery fast.**
- **If you put desires and aspirations ahead of prudence, you will fail.**
- **Poor planning makes you vulnerable.**
- **The more complex your plans, and the longer you try to work outside the boundaries of convention, the greater the likelihood that you will fail.**

I encourage you to give serious thought to what I have written. Do not delude yourself into believing that you are doing things right by ignoring the warning signs along the way. In the very least, the opportunities for your life will be constricted. Life will be more challenging and less satisfying. Worse, the consequences might be disastrous.

Axioms

These may be read in a matter of minutes, but that is not the objective. The more they are contemplated, the more they strengthen one's understanding of life as it should be.

1. Many people are knowledgeable, few are wise.
2. Not all relationships are worth cultivating; some should be avoided all together.
3. Heed your intuition. It may be wrong, but it does not lie.
4. Don't be afraid to apologize for past mistakes, even ones made long ago, but let go of the past.
5. Everybody fails, some are just more truthful about it than others.
6. Integrity matters, and the more you strive for that, the more you will be challenged in your own life to maintain it.
7. Don't be guilty of a wasted life.
8. Just because something is popular, that does not make it right.
9. Not all things are negotiable. On certain matters there is no room for compromise.
10. People who speak eloquently do not necessarily do so with altruistic motives.
11. You may not like what the Bible says, but there is nothing in it that can be or has been proved wrong.
12. If you don't want trouble in your life, don't let trouble into your life. Keep this in mind regarding whom you befriend and with whom you associate.
13. Every person is my superior in at least one capacity.

A Trifecta

14. Do not ascribe to notions you know to be silly or unsustainable.
15. Don't ignore common sense.
16. Common sense is not all that common (Voltaire, 1694-1778)

17. Some believe the sin is in getting caught, not in the action. You do not want to have close association with such people.
18. Help others when you are able, even sometimes when they are seemingly not deserving. You don't know what else is going on in their life.
19. Make critical decisions based on facts, not emotions.
20. Gather the facts before drawing conclusions.
21. When your suspicions are proved wrong, admit it.
22. Save the drama for Hollywood.
23. In business, best-case scenarios rarely happen, and in reality, worse-case scenarios can be much worse than you have imagined.
24. Pay attention to the details and intricacies of nature. They did not happen by chance.
25. Your reputation goes before you.
26. Persevere through hard times.
27. Avoid greedy people. You may have to contend with them, but you do not want to be subject to them.
28. Grow up; just because something offends you, that does not mean it's not true.

Three Truths

29. The U.S. legal system is the best of any crafted by man.
30. The U.S. legal system is marginal at best. Avoid going to court to the extent you are able.
31. The U.S. legal system is based on rules and precedence. If you go to court seeking fairness and justice you may be disappointed by the outcome.

32. Do not allow legal advice to supersede your own good judgement or integrity.

33. Those who are most boisterous typically are insecure and have the most to hide.

Contentious people:

34. Can play their game better than you can play their game.
35. Will wear you down.

Get them out of your life as fast as possible.

Disingenuous people:

36. ditto 34 above.
37. ditto 35 above.

Get them out of your life as fast as possible.

38. Hardships force you to reassess your priorities and force compromise. Know your limits.
39. Hardships can take a long time to work through. Stay focused, hopeful, and positive.
40. At some point, someone in whom you placed your trust and confidence will violate that trust and confidence. How you deal with this will dictate what you learn from the experience. Be prepared, because it will also shape your character.
41. Do not be ignorant of this fact: The depravity of man is boundless.
42. Speak well of others whenever you are able. Your words will be noted as a reflection of your character.
43. Regardless of external circumstances, keep joy as your companion. (This is sometimes hard to do.)
44. A wave and a smile to a stranger costs nothing, yet may be priceless.
45. Generosity comes in many forms.
46. Life is easier when you are organized.
47. Do not do business with anyone who offers unwarranted or excessive praise or flattery.
48. By your choosing, avoid prideful people. They are fatiguing, and they will wear you down.
49. By your choosing, avoid prideful people. They cannot be trusted to act in your best interest.

50. Contain the prideful people with whom you must contend. Do not allow them to define the rules of conduct or terms of engagement. Do this politely and you will either wear them down or they will go away. Either way, you win.

51. Do not let you own pride get in the way of relationships with others.

52. Be proactive to preclude having to be reactive.

53. Make sure those whom you appreciate know you appreciate them. Tell them with your words and show them with your deeds.

54. Use debt sparingly. Avoid it if you can.

55. Work at maintaining a calm disposition. Emotions cloud both contentious issues and difficult decisions.

56. The solutions to difficult decisions come about only by making hard choices. If this is your obligation you have a duty to yourself and others to follow though.

57. The line between accountability and grace is sometimes hard to discern. When in doubt, better to default toward grace.

58. Do not be naive, believing that man is inherently good will pull you into bankruptcy.

59. Trust and confidence are earned, not given.

60. Certain people can prove themselves to be unbelievable jerks. Politely but firmly do not allow them to set the rules of engagement.

61. Certain people can prove themselves to be unbelievable jerks. Avoid falling into that category.

62. Be willing to stand against the crowd when your position is well founded. Just because 99 people say you are wrong, it does not mean that they are right.

63. The answer to the question never asked is always "No".

64. The danger of verbal agreements is that people tend to hear only what they want to hear. Put important details in writing.

65. Learn as much early in life as you are able. That will help unclutter your future.

66. Any drug use (including marijuana), and excessive alcohol use short circuit opportunities.

67. Be interested in other people:
    - You may learn much from them.
    - You never know how a kind act will come back to benefit you.
    - You may be the source of encouragement someone needs.

Words We May Not Understand

I have a friend who tells the story of a repeated experience when he was an American living in Eastern Europe. People from that country would say to him: "You Americans sing your song 'God Bless America'... What's wrong with you! Don't you realize you have already been blessed beyond measure?" They make a good point. Their understanding of the words may not be quite right, but their point is still a good one, and one worth considering.

For those of us who even know that song, fewer and fewer as our country deviates from the values that made our nation great, most don't recognize it as a prayer of submission and supplication. Yet that is what it is.

> "God bless America, land that I love.
> Stand beside her, and guide her..."

That sounds to me like we're humbly asking for leadership and God's direction, not for more and more stuff.

The correlation is undeniable: Through most of the 20th century and continuing into this present one, the United States was perceived to stand out as a beacon of light and hope for a world that struggled. The light that once shone brightly now grows dimmer as we, individually, collectively, and societally, lose our respect and reverence for God.

So when I see someone piously driving around with a bumper sticker on their car that reads: "God bless all nations, no exceptions" I think: That person does not understand that blessings come only through reverence and submission to God's authority. More caustically I think: That person is a fool and they should go get educated. They are a part of the problem, not the solution.

Then I wonder, have I just poisoned this whole book with such a toxic comment? I brush off that concern with an admonition to those offended to go read axiom 28 found in the previous section of this book, knowing they may come back at me citing axiom 61. Then I have to admit there are times where I can be an unbelievable jerk. In those instances I ask that you forgive me please. I hope that is not my dominant nature.

But give credence to the fact that at the core consideration of this issue I am also right. America would hold a different position on the world's stage if we paid attention to the words of that song.

Uncommon Wisdom

There is a man I know. I will refer to him simply as John Doe. Mr. Doe has more common sense and a better developed work ethic than many people. He is not highly educated, at least not in a formal sense, but he is smarter than most. His wisdom comes from experience, lessons learned, and priorities he has set for his life. John is a teacher, mentor, and counselor. He stands alongside those attempting to escape the world he once lived in, a world that does not readily let go its devotees. I have much respect for this man. Though I have not seen him in years I think of him as a friend.

Consider all that my friend has working against him. Our society readily acknowledges these as things no one should want said about themselves:

* John has the minimum in terms of an acceptable level of education.
* John is a convicted felon.
* John used to be strung out on heroin. He won't say he is a recovered heroin addict, he always uses the verb in a present, active tense. He is a recovering heroin addict, an acknowledgement that his recovery will continue for the rest of his life.

John is also an African-American male. That segment of our population is often slighted by other segments. Though we may not be willing to admit it, our tendency is to "paint with a broad paint brush". We tend to lump those not deserving of an accusation with the deserving, in this case just because of the color of their skin. As a result there are many good, respectable African-American males who get slighted.

Sadly, we can take this one step further. John is a dark-skin black man. Those men tends to receive a greater portion of slighting, abuse, and accusation, even from members of their own race. I find that sad, both on a broad scale and as it affects individuals. John is a friend, and he is a good man.

For a period of time I had the opportunity to work alongside Mr. Doe. He earned my respect as a reliable contractor on several construction projects I managed. I will always remember one conversation we had. It let me know John is wiser than most by many measures.

One day as we spoke casually the topic of conversation turned to core beliefs and what it is that gives meaning to life. John's statement struck me as profound: "You can believe in whatever you want to believe in" he said. "But whatever it is that you make to be your god, make sure it's big enough so no one can take it from you." Continuing, and pointing to a nearby chair, he said: "You can make that chair your god if you want to, but if someone comes and takes that chair away, you are in trouble. Whatever it is you make to be your god, make sure it's big enough that no one can take it from you."

Wow, I thought, this guy gets it. This man, whom many would look down on, has greater comprehension of a very important matter than most do. With simple words he cut through the folly of so many people's misguided beliefs. In just a few sentences he summed up several big truths:

- It is easy to get distracted and place higher importance on certain things than they rightfully deserve. In so doing, those things become someone's god.
- If someone can fully describe their god, then they have simple beliefs and their god is not very big.
- If someone's concept of god is based only on emotion and feelings, then their god is not very big, and it can be taken from them.
- Any god that can be taken from you will not be there to sustain you through hard times.

John understands the difference between big "G" and little "g": God, not god.

As we continued to talk there was a radio playing in the background and a commercial came on for (a well known and expensive drug rehab clinic). John stopped and listened, laughed, and said: "The Ottawa County Jail was my (drug rehab clinic).

How can you not like a guy like this? Honest, unassuming, one who holds no pretenses and doesn't care what others think about him. I would like to have more people like that in my life.

Thank you Mr. Doe for setting yourself to be a good example to others. Being the modest man you are, you may not even realize how you influence people who are struggling; people in need of reason and guidance.

I doubt Mr. Doe knows who Blaise Pascal is, but I suspect he agrees with one of his statements: "The heart has its reasons which reason cannot know."

So let me ask you, what is it that you have made to be your god? Is it big enough that no one can take it from you? When the storms of life come abruptly upon you will your beliefs and your god be sufficient to hold you secure?

I encourage you, do not miss the opportunity to have a relationship with the big "G" because you have become so enraptured with a little "g". The little "g"s can and will be taken from you.

Good Idea, Not So Good Idea - Transitioning From the Latter to the Former

I seek to live my life on a higher plane. While maintaining complete emotional detachment I want to observe people and see how they interact with others:

- to identify cause and effect relationships, yet not be affected by anyone's actions.
- to become wise by noting the inclinations of others and cataloging the results those inclinations produce. Perhaps by studying this data I will learn to identify defining characteristics that enable me to predict what any person's inclinations may be, given any situation. Human behavior, after all, is predictable if you understand what it is that compels people to act the way they do.
- to note if and how Newton's Third Law of Motion - *every action has an equal and opposite reaction* - applies to both individuals and society.

Living a life with this grand cosmic overview has great academic appeal, or at least it seems like it should have great academic appeal.

In this utopian world I can look at one man and say: "His decisions and actions cause him to have an unsettled life. He is like the waves of a storm-tossed ocean colliding against a jagged-cliff shoreline." From my observations I would know this individual is unpredictable - sometimes helpful, sometimes an obstruction - a difficult person to contend with over the long-term. This guy isn't the most objectionable type of person to deal with, but he is still fatiguing, a usurper of energy. I won't allow myself to think: "If only he would see things differently" because:

A) he won't see things differently, he is who he is / he is what he is; and

B) that would mean I have attached emotion to the situation, and my envisioned utopia does not allow that. Besides, there are plenty of "if only" situations.

Rather than get emotional I am better off maintaining my detached poise. Serious academic studies do not allow emotions to cloud issues. Things are what they are; nothing more, nothing less.

My attention could then turn to another, and my observations would reveal the person made poor choices earlier in life. As a result those choices have restricted him in any number of ways. Perhaps he is a decent-enough guy who got a girl pregnant when they were both teenagers. Now, instead of going to college, he slaves away at a low-income hourly wage job to provide for an unintended family, one he may have once aspired to have, but not under these conditions. With the emotional detachment I seek to maintain my journal entry may simply read: "Well, he got what he deserves; actions have consequences."

I could look at the lonely, disheartened, disenfranchised, or those who have been beaten down in life, and in my pursuits catalog how these people respond to situations. My observations may also reveal how opportunity-limiting events and decisions are brought upon them due to their vulnerabilities. My journal entries for these folks would be short and to the point. Observing their hardships would be taxing to my quest for emotional detachment.

As a counterbalance I would then need to direct my observations to someone who lives a serene life, comfortable, and able to contend with whatever situation they find themselves in. These folks are much easier to observe academically: lilly white, squeaky clean, everything's rosy; nothing to challenge emotional detachment.

But here is the rub: I do not want to be the type of person who would choose to live their life devoid from the emotional attachment to others. I have witnessed people like that and have seen how their self-absorption makes them callous to the needs of others. I have had to contend with people like that, and suffered loss, because their self-importance is fed at the expense of others. I do not want to become a person like that. They are strongly shielded from pain and hurt, but they are hollow, and they are not nice people. They are more fatiguing to contend with than any others.

So maybe I need to rethink my original premise.

I seek to live my life on a higher plane: to be an observer of human nature so I better understand what compels people to do the things they do; to be empathetic to peoples' hardships and be willing to help where I am able; but to be wise, so my energy is not usurped by those who gladly take at the expense of others and seldom, often never, think to give anything in return.

Yup... that seems like a better approach.

Wealth Beyond Measure

I have a friend whom I have known for more than forty years. I don't get to see her much because she lives out West. She doesn't come back to Michigan very often, and I have gone to visit her only one time. That was years ago when she provided the accommodations for another friend and I to ski down some really steep, snowy mountains. Still, I count her one of my closest and dearest friends.

Life has been hard on my friend. She was married once and she has a daughter from that relationship whom she loves very much. Her marriage did not last. The aging process took a premature toll on my friend's body, so she has endured many years of compromised health, chronic pain, and physical limitations. That, in turn, has limited her ability to earn an income. She has survived, but has never experienced financial abundance. To her credit she takes it all in stride and doesn't complain. My friend is a Christian and has apparently learned how to live as the Apostle Paul[33] wrote: to be content "in plenty or in want."[34]

---

[33] A quick Bible lesson: The Bible is composed of 66 separate books and letters. 39 of the books were written before the time of Jesus. These are referred to as the Old Testament. The remaining 27 books (letters) were written after Jesus' death. These are referred to as the New Testament. "Apostle" is a title ascribed to leaders of the early church - the years immediately following Jesus' death - men who personally knew Jesus and were appointed by him to tell folks how to find favor with God. Paul was one of those guys. Paul wrote 13 of the 27 letters contained in the New Testament. When you read and understand about Paul's experiences in his life as an apostle you realize that his claim of contentment in plenty or in want is quite remarkable.

[34] Reference Philippians 4: 11-12 (NIV)

There is a quality that sets my friend apart from anyone else I know. She intentionally invests herself in the lives of others. Through her actions she lets others know she cares about them. My friend pays attention to, and makes note of, the dates and special occasions that others celebrate as part of their lives. Without fail, for those whom she holds dear, she makes a point to send notes to acknowledge birthdays, anniversaries; Christmas greetings, and other meaningful events. No doubt she has a calendar that has every day full of reminders and remembrances to keep track of dates that have meaning to others.

My wife and others whom I know make similar claims about my friend.

Of this I am quite certain: My friend has invested herself in the lives of so many people that she could walk down any road - from coast to coast, or from the borders of Canada to the Gulf of Mexico - and at the end of the day there would be someone there waiting with an open door and a smile on their face to welcome her in for the evening.

My friend doesn't have much money, but by other standards she has wealth beyond measure. Through her generosity she uses what she has to enrich the lives of others. In that capacity she has given to me in plenty.

Screwing Up Before Sun Up

No guilt trip, just an honest assessment.

So where to begin? Face obstacles head on I always say, and do the difficult tasks first while you have the energy to do so. That will make the other stuff easier to do later. Here goes:

I do not like to admit it but I screw up. Sometimes I screw up in big ways and sometimes in little ways. I'm not thinking so much about minor indiscretions, like grabbing the biggest piece of pie when sitting at a table with others. The threat of ridicule is usually a sufficient deterrent to keep me from doing that. I'm thinking about screw ups that reveal what it is that I consider to be important.

These are test-of-character issues and I failed. Some events I can attribute to external pressures, and others to me being put in a tenuous situation by someone else's actions. Those are not sufficient excuses though. No excuses are sufficient. I am not obligated to screw up or fall short because of someone else's actions. Honesty compels me to admit, too, that there are some shortcomings that fall into the "I don't care, I'm going to do it my way regardless of how it affects others" category.

I am not here to make excuses nor am I inclined to reveal the details. This is a time for introspection. Its purpose is for me to face the fact that there may be a disparity between the person I am and the person I purport myself to be.

This isn't self-flagellation, it is introspection; taking time to assess how I live my life in comparison to how I say I live my life. A desire for continuous improvement.

The good news is that I am now less prone to be guilty of these shortcoming than I was at an earlier time in life. Gratefully I can't think of any issues on the current calendar. But still, I know the history is there.

Why bother with this self-subjected inquisition? Because I know me and I know what I am capable of. The way I term it is: "On any given occasion I can screw up a dozen different ways before sun up." I am not malicious or deceitful, I don't lie or steal, but I do have my foibles. So this is just a reality check, an opportunity for evaluation and correction if needed.

I prefer to discipline me rather than give someone else a reason to discipline me. Quite frankly, it is less embarrassing if I do this this way.

By my line of reasoning I never want to purposefully do anything that would embarrass my wife or children. So maybe I can say, too, that I am doing this for selfish reasons... and in this case, there is nothing wrong with that.

One other reason for the reality check is that I aspire to live a disciplined life and be a man of integrity; one who is more concerned about helping others than always watching out for just myself. I have read about people who have committed themselves to these standards of living, and I admire them for their sense of duty and honor. There was a movie once made about such a guy. His name was Brian Piccolo and the title of the movie is <u>Brian's Song</u>.

Brian Piccolo was a running back for the Chicago Bears football team from 1965 through 1969. He died at the young age of 26 from a fast-growing cancer. While a member of the Bears, and earlier at Wake Forrest where he attended college, he did what he could to edify and benefit others. Brian lived his life exercising a discipline referred to as "I am third." With explanation in terms of priorities: God and family are first, others are second, I am third.

Some think of this as a foolish way to live life. I do not fall into that category. I see a preponderance of evidence that affirms you get more from doing things for others than if you are only concerned about the proverbial numero uno. The rewards do not necessarily come through material or financial gains, but by giving to others it seems that you get more than if you just keep all for yourself. I like that.

Earning Another's Trust

How ironic. My plan for this essay was to write about an author whose works I have enjoyed reading. The man died many years ago, yet his books remain popular. The writer had a gift for storytelling. With references cited I assumed the facts of his stories were presented appropriately. As I gathered background information, however, I discovered the author's accuracy of pertinent details had been called into question. The author was also accused of embellishing the truth regarding the extent of relationships he maintained with prominent people. Repeated acts of plagiarism was another charge leveled against the man. So now I am challenged with a new perspective. I have learned much from the author, and the controversies do not make him a bad man, but I don't want to present him here as the role model I once thought he was.

Following my discovery I first thought to simply delete this topic from the Table of Content. Problem solved. However, upon further consideration I realized there are two great issues to note: the first being whom do you trust; the second, how quickly trust can disappear.

So whom do I trust, the author or the background source? Because I can't say one or the other definitively, neither gets mentioned by name. The source is often cited, yet readily admits it is fallible. Accuracy is the goal, but slanted views and inaccuracies are not fully avoidable. The source does fact-check information and updates its presentations accordingly, yet lapses occur. I accept the source's explanation of the challenges it faces, and factor that in as I evaluate the quality of information I obtain.

Regarding the author, I shouldn't completely condemn a man when he's not here to defend himself. His response to one controversy that arose prior to his death was plausible, but subsequent issues should not be ignored. As before, it is appropriate to factor all available information into my assessment.

I am periodically reminded that a healthy dose of skepticism is worth having. That may stand contrary to my inclinations - wanting to believe the best in people - but starting with that prevents embarrassment later. Skepticism does not mean I have to live my life with a negative outlook. It does mean, however, that I will not blindly accept as true everything that other people say. Taking time to verify information gives me both the basis and confidence to defend my position if the need later arises.

So then, pertaining to more personal and critical issues, whom do you trust? Whom can you trust? One adage to remember is that trust is earned, not given. That is appropriate. It means there is a time element involved. Longevity and consistency are key components of earning trust: consistently following through on your word and keeping commitments; consistently doing the next right thing, whatever that may be; consistently keeping confidence. These are the actions that build trust, the actions you should be looking for in others. In similar fashion others will be watching to see if you possess those qualities. Proverbially speaking, trust is a two-way street.

There are varying degrees of trust to consider, too. Any successful business person may tell you they trust their employees to do their jobs well. They will likely tell you also that they had to hire and fire many employees to ferret out those not deserving of trust.

That employer will also rely on their attorney and accountant to make sure business and tax related issues are dealt with properly. The circle of this second group is smaller, and the level of trust greater.

Note, too, the distinction between expectation and trust: I expect many people to do various things; the number of people I trust implicitly, though, are very few. That should be true for you as well.

When expressed confidence is violated trust quickly disappears. The old adage is: 1 "oh darn it" will undo 100 "atta-boys." With very few exceptions, once trust is broken it takes a long time to rebuild. Forgiveness may come soon, but forgetting a transgression takes longer. People need to be mindful of this as they choose how to live their lives, and as they consider in whom they will put their trust.

Talk is cheap, and actions speak louder than words. Your actions will reveal to others whether you are trustworthy. Likewise, other's actions will reveal the same about them to you.

Possessing the character traits that affirm you to be a trustworthy person is admirable. It comes about through the life you choose to live, the priorities you set, and the decisions you make every day.

Notes to Self

I am thinking I need to be a bit more stoic. Not standoffish, rather just a bit less obvious in expressing my emotions. It is not essential that the whole world be aware of what I am thinking. As is, anyone who cares to watch will readily know when I am angry. Those are the times where I write things like:

- Never never never never never never give up.
- Never never never never never never compromise the truth.
- Never never never never never never let someone talk you into doing something you know is not the right thing to do.
- With very few exceptions, never never never never never never believe someone will earnestly work with your best interest in mind, even though they profusely profess that they will.

While three "never(s)" are usually sufficient for most folks I feel compelled to double the amount. I wonder why that is? Still, those points are valid and prudent rules to live by.

Maybe, I am thinking, I stand too close to certain issues. There are only a few things I have the ability to control, so I shouldn't get wrapped up in the details of issues where I have no influence. That seems prudent.

I just had a couple more thoughts: I should learn to laugh more often, and smile; be kind when I feel like being vindictive. Those seems like good rules to live by, too.

Why hold onto anger and aggravation? You can find humor in most situations, even if it's just being bemused by the folly and insane foolishness of others, or the gallows humor that comes with hearing some incredibly stupid opinion expressed by someone who holds a position of power. You might as well laugh rather than get bent out of shape if its one of those situations you have no control over. There is a title to a song that seems to apply here: <u>Things That Make You Go Hmmm</u>. Hmmm.

Well, this has been an interesting exercise. I was angry when I started, the never never never(s) came first. The words preceding and those that follow were added later. All told I probably spent no more than twenty minutes writing. Now I feel better; no more frumping around. I would call that twenty minutes well spent.

These new revelations and decisions do not mean that I am not concerned. They just mean I need to be cognizant of boundaries. Like Dirty Harry, a tough guy from the movies, says: "A man's got to know his limitations."

Exit laughing.

Same Story, Different Audience

If you have a genuine concern for other people there are few jobs more rewarding than that of being a teacher. As part of your daily obligations you have the opportunity to interact with others in a positive and edifying manner. For those under your administration you have the chance to broaden their horizons, provide information to enable them to gain a proper perspective on critical issues, and offer words of encouragement that may propel them further than they would otherwise go. For these reasons and more I found life on a university campus as a lecturer to be very enjoyable. There is one anecdote from that time in my life that I want to share with you.

Though my topics of lecture pertained to corporate finance and personal investments, as time allowed I would take tangential opportunities to discuss issues my students would encounter once they entered the working world. This, I believe, provided more complete information: topic, comprehension, and perspective.

One day I was with my brother, someone whom I did not often get to see, and I told him of a recent class session. In my lecture I talked about the 1973 movie Papillon. Steve McQueen and Dustin Hoffman were the stars of the movie, both of whom were popular actors in that era. The story pertains to a man named Henri Charriere, an inmate of a penal colony located on Devils Island, French Guyana.

Though a career criminal, the story line says Henri was wrongfully accused of the crime that sent him to the brutal environment of that remote, isolated location. In one scene, having been subject to harsh physical treatment, extended solitary confinement, and near starvation, Henri began to hallucinate:

> The environment of the hallucination was stark, barren, and desolate. On one edge stood Henri; on the other, separated by some distance, was a tribunal of judges seated behind a podium on a raised platform. Once aware of their presence Henri starts to walk toward them proclaiming: "I'm not guilty! It's not my fault! I didn't do it!" At the same time the chief judge bangs his gavel and says: "We find you guilty..."
>
> The banter goes back and forth as Henri gets closer: "I'm not guilty! It's not my fault! I didn't do it!"; "We find you guilty..."
>
> With each repetition Henri gets more adamant and agitated, and continues right to the point where he is standing at the base of the judges' bench. One last time Henri proclaims: "I'm not guilty..." The judge cuts him short, bangs his gavel, and says: "We find you guilty... of a wasted life." Upon hearing those final words Henri turned around, hung his head low, and walked away with shame saying: "Guilty, guilty, guilty."

I told that story to my students as an admonition. The goals and ideals of youth can give way to either self-serving attitudes with little regard for the concern of others, or defeat for those whose path through life turns hard. Sometimes those outlooks creep into people's life surreptitiously and without their knowing, and neither are beneficial nor desirable. I told this story because I hoped that my students would experience satisfying futures, and I did not want any of them to be guilty of a wasted life.

When I finished talking my brother said he knew the scene and verbal exchange well, and it was one he also often cited. My brother, a Circuit Court judge, said he would tell the same story to some of those who appeared before him in his courtroom. Convicted of their crimes, he would tell people the story of Henri Charriere right before he sent them to prison. (Wow, I thought at the time, his story is better than mine; he wins.)

My brother used the story as a source of encouragement. Those who were convicted had to pay the penalty for their transgressions. Their past, though, did not need to define their future. Once their sentence was served they could change, and not be guilty of a wasted life.

Same story, same lesson, different reasons.

What ever the future holds for you, good or bad; pleasant or a hard struggle, I implore you, do not be guilty of a wasted life.

Bub

Bub is something of a ubiquitous term in my vernacular. I use it all the time in greetings, salutations, and casual conversation. "Hey bub"... "Whatcha doin' bub"... "Pay attention bub", are all expressions you may hear me say. I don't recall ever calling a girl or lady bub so I guess it's a term I use only with the male gender of our species. Bub connotes familiarity, so I use the term only with guys with whom I have an established relationship. I would not, for example, use the term bub when talking with the President of the United States.

There is one person for whom the word bub needs to be written as first-letter capitalized - Bub. He is a guy with whom I have an in-depth friendship, and I call him Bub more frequently than I use his given name.

Bub is a protector, a term often confused with, but significantly different from the words aggressor and warrior. Bub won't start a fight, but he won't run from one either. He doesn't need to prove himself, so that gives him the freedom to try and diffuse situations before they become excessively contentious. Bub will take a punch before he throws a punch, but an uninformed aggressor may quickly find out that Bub was trained as a pugilist and is still, even at his current age, fully capable of defending himself and others. An aggressor coming up against Bub may literally get an education of hard knocks.

At an earlier station in life Bub got to experience overseas travel of a kind the sane would not look forward to. He didn't look forward to it, but he did what he had to do out of duty and obligation. Bub endured some of the most fierce battles of a very brutal and unpopular Asian war. He did what the situation required him to do, got Agent Orange dumped on him, and survived. Upon his return to The States he had to endure all the slanderous, contentious verbal assaults that the arrogant condescending youth of the times heaped upon our soldiers. Many of that arrogant crowd are now in positions of authority and influence in our government, which helps explain why we are in the mess we are in.

Thirty years passed between that earlier era and when I first met Bub. We have similar interests and both of us enjoy the satisfaction that comes with the accomplishments of hard physical work, so there is much commonality between us. As our friendship developed I realized we have similar perceptions of the world around us, and we share a desire of wanting to help others in need.

Several years ago Bub sorted through some issues tied to his earlier-life's experiences. He took a proactive approach and went to talk with psychiatrists at the Veteran's Administration. He found a team of specialists who helped him quantify issues and put them in their proper perspective. Through a series of meetings they articulated and explained the distinctions between protector and aggressor, and affirmed Bub as the former. As he told me about his meetings the thought I had was that the VA folks were saying things I knew about him all along, but never thought to tell him. It's a good thing he worked with the VA doctors, though. They have referent, professional, and positional authority that I do not have.

How was it that I knew the issues concerning Bub's character? I read about him in a book that was written several thousand years ago, the first book of Samuel, one of the books that comprise the Old Testament of the Bible.

First Samuel, chapter 17 records the account of a fight between two guys, David and Goliath. At the time of the encounter David was relatively young, probably a teenager. Verse 42 of chapter 17 describes him as "ruddy and good looking." Most likely he was physically fit, but his stature wouldn't win a bodybuilding competition. David's day-job was to take care of his family's flock of sheep. David was the youngest of his father's sons, which in the pecking-order of the times probably put him at the bottom of the proverbial totem pole. I suspect David was likable and easy to get along with, but also someone who held firm to his convictions. Goliath, conversely, was a loudmouthed and bombastic aggressor. Physically Goliath was huge; professionally he was a seasoned and battle-tested warrior. He intimidated everybody, except David, and he reveled in his stature.

The personality traits of the two also provided a stark contrast. Elsewhere in the Bible it says that David sought to honor God. Goliath, conversely, was focused on self-glorification.

On the day that made David famous he wasn't looking to pick a fight. His day began by running an errand for his father. When he was confronted by an untenable situation, however, he was compelled to act for the protection of that which he held dear. The rest of the story and the details of what happened next is history. If you don't know the story find a Bible, or go on line, and read 1 Samuel 17.

The attributes written about David in his encounter with Goliath apply to Bub as well. So when I heard what the VA doctors told him I had two thoughts:

1. I know Bub's character because I recognized it from the description of David.
2. I wonder if the VA doctors read the same ancient books I read because it seems like they recognized Bub's character, too.

There is a great quote attributed to Winston Churchill that fits well: "We sleep safely at night, because rough men stand ready to visit violence on those who would harm us." I am glad there are people like Bub. They make the world, and my community, a safer place.

The Songbird Cafe

In the midst of one of America's most dilapidated cities sits one of the best restaurants you could hope to find. The fare is casual and the menu sufficiently diverse; the quality is topnotch, and the hours of operation long. For the proprietors, a husband and wife tagteam, the workday starts with early morning breakfast preparation and continues through the day, concluding with meals for the late-night crowd. Friday night and Saturday night have extended hours for the ridiculously late-night crowd. The restaurant is closed on Sunday, a day of rest for everyone.

The business now works sufficiently well so the proprietors are in the position to shift some responsibilities to a couple trusted employees. Their main cook (a nice guy and the best grill man I have ever met) is devoted to doing his job well. His commitment makes life easier for the owners. Other employees treat their jobs with a commensurate level of dedication, and work in similar fashion to ensure the business thrives. Its success and prosperity translate into their success and prosperity.

The restaurant is located near the boundaries of ghetto-quality real estate. It has an interesting mix of staff and clientele, and most of the employees come from the lower socio-economic class. The point here is not where they come from, but where they are going. The proprietors are not just concerned about running a for-profit business, they are concerned as well about teaching others how to get out of poverty and realize life's potential. In an informal yet exacting manner the employees learn the essentials to move themselves forward.

This is really an interesting point when you stop and think about it. Through the benefit of their jobs the employees receive more than just a paycheck. There are non-monetary benefits that come with their employment. The owners, because of their concern for others, teach:

- Personal care and hygiene - wash your face; brush your teeth; make sure your hair is combed or nicely styled; wear clean, properly fitting clothes (no baseball caps, nor saggy pants allowed; anything that suggests gang membership or participation is definitely not allowed).

- Self respect - no drugs allowed, never ever ever. The owners have seen the deprivation that comes with excessive alcohol use so they advocate abstention. That is one way they express concern for their employees.

- Communication skills - speak clearly and enunciate; speak precisely (no slang); look people in the eyes; smile.

- Responsibility and team work - be attentive to your work schedule; show up for work on time; be ready to work when your shift starts; be helpful; be cheerful.

- Look toward the future - apply everything you are learning; set goals; achieve.

The owners are courteous, but demanding. Any employee who comes to work with a bag full of excuses will not remain an employee for long. Allowing them to remain would destroy work crew morale, and it would not be fair to others who strive to achieve.

Because of its proximity to the poor side of town many of the restaurant's clientele come from there. The restaurant sits on a major thoroughfare though, so it also draws clientele from more affluent areas. The commingling of diverse socio-economic groups does not cause any issues; the owners will not allow it.

The Songbird Cafe is really a great American success story. The owners aren't bazillionaires, but the business affords them a comfortable living. It provides them the opportunity to help others, too. This couple came out of a rough & tumble background. They know the hardships of poverty, and they decided long ago that was not where they wanted to live their lives. Their success story is twenty years in the making.

When the restaurant first opened the owners faced many hurdles. The banks would not lend them money because restaurants have a notoriously high failure rate and banks know this. So the Mr. worked two other jobs plus the cafe obligations as time would allow, while the Mrs. kept the continuity of their goals on course. The banks not lending them money is not necessarily a bad thing. Borrowed money can work against you in ways more damaging than it can work for you. The absence of cash reserves forced them to be disciplined in their expenditures. They had yet to establish accounts with wholesale food brokers, and I recall times where I watched them make a quick dash to the grocery store to stock up on essentials as inventories ran precariously low. This happened with a certain amount of regularity. It wasn't ideal, but it enabled the proprietors to manage their resources in an efficient manner.

Persistence, careful planning, and dutiful efforts paid off. The owners recently remodeled the restaurant and expanded its seating area, a testament to hard work, perseverance, and a job well done. Hooray for the Songbird Cafe!

Several blocks away there sits a facility in contrast to The Songbird. The building is one of the nicest in the area, it houses the Department of Social Services (DSS). It has a clientele much larger than that of the Songbird, but can claim none of the cafe's successes. DSS is not meant to lift people out of poverty; it locks them in and keeps them there.

There are stark contrasts between the Songbird and DSS. Just as the owners of the cafe know, I understand there is a segment of our society that needs help and assistance. That segment though, has been allowed (and perhaps encouraged) to become generational. That presents a variety of problems, and it is not fair to many. The motivation may be just, but the outcomes are predominantly wrong.

DSS may provide an essential service, yet I have heard comments from members of the community who resent its presence and method of operations. Their staffing consists of well-paid government employees from outside the community who prosper at the expense of the poor. That is a legitimate indictment. There comes a time where it is appropriate to ask: Whom are they really aiding, and would the Songbird Cafe approach work better?

Peripheral Vision and Loss Thereof

The flight left at 12:40 a.m., at which point we were into the 20th hour of our day. Flight time was something like 11 hours 44 minutes, but when you add in the minutes before "wheels up" and after "wheels down" our time on the plane crowded the 13 hour mark. Ground delays added to the count, and by the time we got through U.S. Customs we missed our connecting flight.

That sort of stuff happens and I'm not complaining about the events or the airlines. We were quite pleased by how accommodating the airline's staff was at getting us to our next destination. The revised plans required that we first get to a different airport, so they arranged transportation and gave us meal vouchers since we still had four hours of down-time before the next flight left. We arrived in Detroit about six hours behind schedule and still had seven hours' worth of obligations before getting to the place we planned to lay our heads for the night. A tight schedule would not accommodate further delay, so we simply committed ourselves to doing what it took to get where we were going.

The last hour of drive time was harder than any I remember. At that point it was 46 hours and counting of being awake, with only a few hours dozing, either on the plane or while someone else drove. Dozing, in either of those conditions, does not count as bonafide sleep. To stay awake I turned down the temperature to put a chill in the car, turned up the radio, and periodically slapped my face to stimulate the senses.

I've driven the roads innumerable times and I know them well. We were in the backwoods of Northern Michigan where we rarely see cars that time of night. That alleviated part of my concern. It was raining, and thinking that wildlife hunker down in such conditions, I wasn't too concerned about deer darting in front of me. My biggest concern was having an intimate encounter with one of the trees alongside the road, and I knew that would not be a good thing. That concern helped keep me attentive.

As we approached the final stretch of road I became increasingly aware of my loss of peripheral vision. Though I thought the potential for wildlife encounter slight I wanted to stay on guard. Every few moments I'd glance from side to side to take note of the broad surroundings. With our destination in sight I could finally relax. We closed out the 47th hour as our heads hit the pillows.

That was a week ago and I'm still adjusting to being back in my preferred time zone. Having returned from the East my tendency is to wake up early - three or four o'clock(ish) - which I don't find to be all that objectionable. I like the hours of early morning. It is a quiet time of solitude and it gives me time to think in detail. It is a time where I am able to connect dots that might not otherwise get connected. Hence, this morning I was thinking about the loss of peripheral vision and another optometric condition, myopia - nearsightedness. Both conditions prevent one from fully observing their surroundings. When applied to a broader consideration, both conditions limits the amount of knowledge that may be gleaned and the depth of understanding that goes with that associated knowledge.

Clear vision, with the benefit of peripheral and absence of myopia, makes you aware in several unrelated capacities:

- It gives you a broad perspective of your surroundings and enables you to see in expanse and detail, a big-picture perspective.
- It provides an early warning for oncoming danger.
- It augments your appreciation for, and understanding of, complex issues.

In certain situations vision unencumbered by limitations enables you to identify cause and effect relationships. When encumbered with limitations you focus on a single point and miss everything around you.

Some may argue that it is the essential issue you should focus on anyway and therefore peripheral vision, or depth of vision, is a secondary consideration. In opposition I will argue that if you narrow your focus down far enough you won't really know what you are looking at. You'll miss out on the understanding that comes with assessing everything as a whole. With just a narrow focus you can present whatever you want to be true as truth: Narrow your focus and define tight parameters, use a select metric or points of affirmation, ignore or be completely unaware of every other consideration, and the delusion begins.

That reality fits well with several definitions provided in Webster's Dictionary for myopia:
- lack of foresight or discernment;
- narrow-mindedness;
- intolerance.

Losing sight of the forest for the trees, I believe, is a polite colloquialism used to describe this situation. Those seem like good things to avoid.

Now I am given pause to think in more detail. I need to clarify in my mind to whom it is that I am writing, and to clearly identify the salient point(s) that need to be articulated.

The premise on which I started was based on the assumption that this essay might have most meaning for people of a younger generation, say, the under-30 crowd. Its purpose was to make them aware of changes in societal norms they may not be aware of. In regard to morals and societal standards, the environment they have grown up in and accept as normal is not the same as what existed earlier in our country's history. My concern is that, as a result of these changes, we have both weakened the fabric of society that creates stability, and have lessened the opportunity for future generations to advance and prosper.

As I sought to identify my target market it occurred to me that the opportunity to learn is never limited to any one group. On a grander scale, there are issues we all should consider for the benefit of making wise decisions today (this current time), with a desire to improve the future.

The purpose of this essay is not just to address a specific issue or situation, it is meant to highlight the value of looking at generally accepted principles and asking:

"What if, what more, what am I not seeing?"

"Is there more to the story than what is being told?"

The benefit of this approach is that it enables any individual to develop an inquisitive nature. There is good reason to do that because the rhetorical answer to the second question can be short-circuited by ingrained perspectives and presumed values, a mindless glossing-over of salient points. A better approach is to evaluate situations clearly based on all the facts, with no assumptions or limitations.

There is an often cited quote that applies to this essay: "Those who fail to learn from history are destined to repeat it." That is a paraphrase of a statement originally made by George Santayana, a man whose life spanned portions of the 19th and 20th centuries. Drawing on information taken from Wikipedia, his statement reads:

> "Progress, far from consisting in change, depends on retentiveness. When change is absolute there remains no being to improve and no direction is set for possible improvement; and when experience is not retained, as among savages, infancy is perpetual. *Those who cannot remember the past are condemned to repeat it.*"

Wow, did you catch the significance of that first sentence? Retentiveness is the key; the hinge point around which everything should pivot. We so often think of change as a total abandonment of the past, but that is not how it should be according to Santayana. Do that, he effectively says, and you are throwing the proverbial baby out with the bath water. We may make things different, but we do not necessarily make things better. That is a good lesson to keep in mind the next time some clown comes around talking about hope and change.

Again relying on Wikipedia, other paraphrases of Santayana's statement are:
- Those who cannot learn from history are doomed to repeat it.

- Those who do not remember their past are condemned to repeat their mistakes.
- Those who do not read history are doomed to repeat it.
- Those who fail to learn from the mistakes of their predecessors are destined to repeat them.
- Those who do not know history's mistakes are doomed to repeat them.

They all say the same thing, but sometimes hearing (or reading) different words add clarity and emphasis.

It is all a matter of perspective, and the underlying theme of Santayana's statement is an admonition that encourages us to gather full and complete information. If you don't have full information you know neither where you have come from, nor where you are going.

To reinforce this point two other quotes are worth considering in conjunction with that of Santayana:

- "People will not look forward to posterity, who never look backward to their ancestors." - Edmund Burke, a 19th century Irish statesman
- "The farther backward you can look, the farther forward you are likely to see." - Winston Churchill, Prime Minister of Great Britain during World War II

The three quotes share a common theme. They all advise against living only for today. With strong justification they offer this admonition: You need to know the past, and you need to plan for (and in so-doing, shape) the future.

Consideration of those quotes incline me to believe now is a good time to discuss pivotal issues that affect our society. There are several issues that readily come to my mind. As you think about the ones I cite you are free to add any you deem equally important.

It is not mandatory that you agree with the premises I put forth. An important aspect of this exercise though, is that you should not allow yourself to think only in terms of being for or against, agreeing or disagreeing. Apply Santayana's admonition: "Those who fail to learn from history..." and Churchill's encouragement: "The farther backward you can look..." Deconstruct your thoughts and work back to the core issues so you can explain (to yourself, primarily) why you believe as you do.

On that premise here are some issues I think about and the conclusions I have drawn:

Abortion Rights: Many people have strong opinions regarding this issue, but I doubt many have an understanding of how the procedure became legal in the United States, or how the rules for determination and acceptability have changed over time. With synoptic information obtained from Wikipedia, read, please, where this began:

> *Roe v. Wade* (1973) was a landmark decision by the United States Supreme Court on the issue of abortion. The Court ruled that a right to privacy extended to a woman's decision to have an abortion, but that this right must be balanced against the government's two legitimate interests in regulating abortions: protecting prenatal life and protecting women's health. Arguing that these interests [State's interests] became stronger over the course of a pregnancy, the Court resolved this balancing act by limiting the legal availability of abortion to the first trimester of pregnancy.

The Court later reconsidered *Roe*'s trimester limitation, but affirmed the Decision's core tenet that a woman has a right to an abortion until the fetus is "viable". *Roe* defined viable as being "potentially able to live outside the mother's womb, albeit with artificial aid", adding that viability "is usually placed at about seven months (28 weeks) but may occur earlier, even at 24 weeks."

Disregard the emotions attached to this issue for the moment, and spend time thinking about both the logic and the application of that decision:

- <u>The right to have an abortion, balanced against the State's interests</u> I have a concern: Do we not have a Bill of Rights for the specific purpose of protecting individuals against the intrusion of the government under a nefarious guise of "interests"? That does not seem like a valid standard for determination, because consistency of the law's enforcement cannot be achieved. It becomes a standard that is based on the moving target of emotion and popular opinion.
- <u>The State's interests become stronger</u> Really? The States's interests become stronger as the pregnancy progresses(?) That seems as stupid as saying a woman is a little bit pregnant at the onset, but becomes more pregnant as the child grows in her womb.
- <u>Protect prenatal life</u> Abortions bring about an abrupt end to prenatal life and everything that would follow thereafter. Why do we treat this so lightly?

Now think of the application of that decision as it stands today:

<u>Viability</u> With the medical advances of the last forty years the viability of life outside the womb occurs at a much earlier time in the pregnancy. So on the basis of the original arguments should that not constrain the legal time of allowing the procedure? Yet we have societally expanded the allowable time for an abortion to extend right up to that preceding the moment of birth. (Go read about late-term partial birth abortions if you doubt that statement, and pay particular attention to the gore that procedure entails.)

<u>The uncomfortable conflict with other laws</u> Every state has had to face the issue of what occurs when a pregnant woman is murdered. The perpetrator is typically charged with two felony counts - one on behalf of the woman, the other on behalf of the fetus, the child she carried in her womb. So is that not an admission that the fetus is a separate living human being, even if it is not yet "viable"? To avoid the potential embarrassment caused by this situation many legislators have simply written new laws that identify the murdered fetus as a separate legal entity, but not an official human.

Do these things not strike you as foolish and hypocritical? They certainly do me.

There are other considerations of the abortion issue as well:

- Has the unlimited availability of abortion lessened the perceived value of human life? The short answer has to be yes, and no long answer is needed.

- Has the availability of abortions made us into a more misogynistic society? I think so. We have devalued our societal respect for womanhood. The norms of society used to be such where women were better protected by practiced mores, but we don't do much of that anymore.

The reason I asked you to separate yourself from the emotions of this issue is so you can think clearly without the limiting factor of tunnel vision (emotions). If you concentrate on just the facts, gross hypocrisy seems like a fitting term to use; the promulgation of lies of an incredible magnitude.

I believe this law that was deigned to help women has done the opposite. We have denigrated our respect for life, womanhood, and motherhood. We have lost much as a result. The ambient level of risk that women face today is now much greater than it used to be.

Casinos and Gambling: You can spend your money however you want. I don't much care. To live in community, however, we are not allowed the luxury of thinking only of ourselves. Concerning this matter of legalized gambling the questions I always think of are:

- Why is gambling, which includes state lotteries, always marketed to those who can least afford it?

- If casinos are such a great idea, why do we allow just federally designated Indian tribes - "sovereign nations" is what I hear them referred as - to be the only ones who get to own them? From a business school perspective that is not a legitimate qualification to run a business, let alone an industry.

- Why is it that these sovereign nations can only have casinos on historic tribal land, yet much of the "historic tribal land" happens to be conveniently situated near the ready access of federal highways or in major metropolitan areas?

- Why is there increased crime, and why do other businesses suffer when casinos are built in close proximity to them?
- Why is it that when I'm in a major gambling mecca like Las Vegas I see billboards from loan companies that read "Bring us your car title!"? Do you think that is an indication that there is a problem?

Gosh I hate hypocrisy. You can spend your money however you want, but I think the justifications presented for legalized gambling are a bunch of hooey. I would much prefer that the politicians who vote in favor of legalized gambling tell the truth and admit that by so doing it buys them votes? Gosh I hate hypocrisy.

Legalized Recreational Drug Use: We must be a ship of fools. Stop and think about the seriousness of this issue. Will people achieve their full potential when they are wrecked out of their minds? Is this how we hope to build a nurturing, edifying society? The reality is that if you are not in control of your senses you increase the level of ambient danger to yourself and to those close to you; those close, both in terms of physical proximity and emotional attachment. In not-so-extreme cases also, the dalliances of a person high on drugs, including marijuana, increases the level of obligations that their friends, family and coworkers must endure.

As a side note, only an uninformed or duplicitous fool would argue that recreational drug use is no more harmful than recreational alcohol use.

The Marginalization of Integrity: This may be my greatest concern. It reveals a vulnerability of our society and a weakness in our composite character.

Why do we elect politicians who are less that truthful and those who tell outright lies? Why do we endorse film makers who promote distortions of the truth for self-satisfying reasons? Why do we give prominence to vile charlatans who masquerade as men of God? (I personally believe those guys have an unpleasant fate that awaits them, but in the interim they foment the hostilities of racial divisiveness that plagues our country.) Why do we not hold media sources accountable for their failure to impart information and allow them instead to provide uncontested slanted and biased views? Why can't we have open discussions on controversial issues and not descend into the squalor of vindictiveness and name calling? We can do better. We can do better (repeated intentionally). We can do better, because I believe we are better than what we demonstrate.

I could continue with the list, but that is not the objective. My positions are self-evident and firmly held, but the crux of this essay is outwardly-directed, not inwardly-directed.

It is now your turn. Again, in the absence of emotion, pick your thoughts apart. Answer for yourself how you have arrived at whatever your conclusions may be on critical societal issues, the process you employed for evaluation and consideration. Agree or disagree, either way, use that as a catalyst to get busy. You possess the tools and opportunity to put the outwardly-directed purpose of this essay to work. Pick apart the justifications that are presented to assess the strength of societal positions. Determine whether there is substance or lack thereof. Know what you believe, and know why you believe. Become an activist for truth.

Consider this: Maybe you are the leader, the statesman or stateswoman, we desperately need. There is, at present, a dearth of qualified, bonafide leaders (males and females) who possess the qualities of knowledge, well-based opinions, and integrity, both in the United States and throughout the world; men and women with convictions who know what they believe, know why they believe, and are willing to speak up for the betterment of others.

I encourage you. Maybe we can make our country a better place. If we do that there will be positive, beneficial repercussions throughout the world. My encouragement does come with a warning, though. If you are intent on pursuing truth, and likewise hold the conviction to challenge deleterious societal issues at their root cause, your frustrations may be great. Your satisfactions, however, may be greater.

Boxing legend Muhammed Ali is quoted as having said: "Service to others is the rent you pay for your room here on earth." Perhaps this is your service.

Things You Really Need to Know, And I Said So

Right about now I want to rant. I don't like the trends I see. I don't like the lies politicians and the media tell. I don't like the shortsightedness of people who are too dumb to know better, but they should know better. Nor do I care for their self-serving ways. I have something worthwhile to say that everyone needs to pay attention to. So everyone pay attention! I am going to tell you everything you need to know: how to live, how to eat, with whom to associate and most importantly, how to vote. I have let you have things your way for far too long, and you have totally messed things up. So now it's up to me to straighten things out.

Don't bother taking time to thank me now, save that for later. The more you pay attention to what I say, the more your gratitude for me should grow. You can pay homage to me later. Prior to that time though, be sure to tell all your friends about me. They need to benefit from my wisdom, too, just like you do.

Just think of the multiplying effect that will occur by you telling others about me. (As you know I am an engineer <u>and</u> a math and finance type of guy. I know your respect for me just grew exponentially by me working the words "multiplying effect" into my rant. (*Exponentially* - a math term! Wow, sometimes I even amaze myself! Not only am I all the things I just told you, I am also a wordsmith!)) THIS IS AMAZING! Note, too, the double parentheses "(())". Only engineers know how to use those properly; and math-oriented people. Math-oriented people, which includes science-oriented people know how to use double parentheses properly. Of course, by "science-oriented people" I mean "hard science-oriented people", not "soft science-oriented people" and most definitely not "political science-oriented people" (yuck). It's probably a good thing I stopped and explained that to you.

I realize I haven't expressed these things with quite enough emphasis! I have not yet used nearly enough "!"s to get my point across, and I know you need to look up to me. So for your benefit let me add these: !!. That should be sufficient. Feel free to use those wherever you see fit, and be sure to ask if you are not certain. I will be happy to tell you because, after all, it's very important that you look up to me. But you already know that, or at least you should.

Now, back to that multiplying effect thing: When I tell two people something, and they tell two people, and they tell two people, and on and on, look how my important information gets shared with others:

No. of people I tell something	No. of people they tell what I said	No. of people who now know the important thing I said
2	4	6
	8	14
	16	30
	32	62
	64	126
	128	254
	256	510
	512	1, 022

Do you see how this works? The more people who know the really important things I say, the better things will be.

Here is a good idea, I don't know why I didn't think of this before: tell four people, not just two, and tell the four people you tell to tell four people; and if they are really committed to my important information they don't have to stop at just four. (I shouldn't have to tell you that, you should know it all ready. But you probably don't, so that is why I had to tell you.) The exponential growth will be that much faster and greater. Why, by year's end it may even be possible that all the important people will then know the important things I've said.

Here is another important thing to remember: "important" is a relative term. Don't mess up. **The important thing I said** is <u>more important</u> than the important people who now know **the important thing I said**. This is, after all, all about me, and not about someone else who claims to be important, even if they know **the important thing I said**.

Now it is time to pay the homage to me that I so rightly deserve.

Or maybe these are just the rantings of a raving lunatic.

With exception to the previous sentence that is the creepiest stuff I have ever written. Yet that is how some of us who hold strong opinions on certain subjects, typically morality and politics, come across. Or it may be more appropriate to say, we are accused of coming across that way. People's reactions are based on what they hear; how they interpret certain words. What they want to hear is often a reflection of where their mind and heart is.

I would like to think I have enough sense to keep my mouth shut, and if not, to at least choose my words wisely. In certain circles though, or when around certain groups of people, I don't. I can be as loudmouthed and bombastic as the next guy, perhaps even more so. On the plus side, as if our words get weighed on a balance, I do have strong opinions based on legitimate concerns. Yet is it my opinions I want to express, or an innate desire to tell others that I know more than they do and that I know what is best? Sometimes when I stop and critically assess my position, a deeper issue arises.

There is a quote attributed to Winston Churchill that deals with democracy. It goes something like this: "A five minute conversation with the average voter will confirm any doubts you have about democracy." That guy had a knack for conveying salient points.

The fact is that we do live in an imperfect world. Politicians do lie; the media does slant the truth; people do selfishly vote for the party they believe will benefit them the most; others are totally clueless, but still have a Constitutional right to vote; spinmeisters will convolute the truth, call evil good, and malign the character of good people; and all the while, the sun continues to rise in the morning and set in the evening.

There is a balance to be had, a call to arms, when things get so far out of whack that corrective measures are needed. That typically happens, though not fast enough for some of us when certain people or issues dominate center stage. So being responsible and dutiful is important. This includes being well read on current issues and thinking in broad terms of what best benefits society as a whole. For those of us who profess to be Christians, especially me, the issue goes deeper.

I am going to write the rest of this essay in first-person singular since that is to whom it most aptly applies. If you agree, reading first-person singular applies to you as well. If you don't get what I'm writing about, spend time thinking it over. You may understand having given it some thought.

Whenever I get bent out of shape over political issues or social mores it means I'm not trusting God. Whenever I think of certain politicians, the pronouncements of a particular political party, the lies and deceptions of people who know better, the way the media reports important issues or fails to report them, the chicanery that goes on every day and has for a time longer than I've been around, and most importantly, whenever I let that get me upset and think fleeting thoughts of desired revenge and needed rectification of perceived injustices, I become my biggest problem. (How's that for a run-on sentence?) There are many things I do not have the means to change, but it is not me who is in control either. Nor is it me who needs to be in control. In reality, nor is it me whom I'd want to be in control. I may really screw things up.

Whenever I feel anger or frustration over a situation, or whenever I start to feel contempt toward someone else, I become my biggest problem. I need to step back and create a bit of distance between me and whatever it is I find upsetting. Then I need to tell God about my concerns, and let go. He is the one who lets the world play out as he allows. After all, God has already let me know he has a handle on the situation. Chapter 12 of the book of Daniel, in the Old Testament of the Bible, affirms that God is in control. His knowledge and understanding exceeds mine.

There is a demarkation that needs to be highlighted, i.e., the distinction between acting on convictions, and merely pontificating on less that desirable situations. The former may be how God chooses to effectuate change in a world where change is needed. As was with Daniel, if you have been put in that position nothing can stop you. The latter, however, is ineffectual and petty, merely a rant. It accomplishes nothing.

I am better off if I do not rant. Some issues are not mine to control. An admonition that comes through reading the Book of Proverbs (Old Testament stuff again) is: When there is a fool talking, make sure there isn't a fool listening. I don't want to be on either side of that statement.

Respectfully, We Have Our Rights, Responsibly

We do have our rights. Some are inalienable: life, liberty, civil; and some are granted for the common good: freedom of assembly, freedom of the press, the right to bear arms. These rights grant us freedoms that others long for but will never experience. We should value them and hold them dear.

Pushy and combative people will tell you if they think you have imposed on their rights, yet they typically are not inclined to respect yours. It is sufficiently safe to make a blanket statement regarding these people: They ignore the fact that their rights stop at the point where yours begin. Some folks are annoying that way.

Some people use their determination as the basis of what should be allowed. I am inclined to believe many of the people who express thoughts on what the Founding Fathers "really" intended regarding some of our rights are not highly knowledgeable of that which they speak. Their thoughts are nothing more than opinions based on ill-founded notions. It's a pretty sure bet they have never read any of the important documents that set the framework for our country - Common Sense, The Federalist (Papers), the Declaration of Independence, The Constitution of the United States, the Bill of Rights - nor is it likely they are students of history. Try to take these folks in stride and show compassion on them. They fall into a class of people best described as: "Their arrogance is exceeded only by their arrogance" (I forget who first said that); or as was said of a former female Speaker of the House: "(Their) arrogance is exceeded only by (their) ignorance."

This same crowd often confuses rights with privileges, as in: a "right" to free health care; or a "right" to free education. In so doing they replace appreciation with expectation, usually at someone else's expense. Take pity on these people but don't give them an inch to maneuver. If you do they will take it as a mandate to further bad behavior under the guise of a more altruistic-sounding label.

Those are not the folks I want to talk about though. Let me change course before someone accuses me of being condescending and arrogant.

An important point to discuss is that we do have our rights, but with them come responsibilities. We may even want to consider a variable: The more extensive our rights, the greater our responsibilities. Let's delve into this thought and see where we go with it.

What prompted this essay was an article that appeared in the news recently. Throughout the United States there is an ongoing debate regarding whether people should be allowed to carry firearms openly, as in walk down the street or into a store with a holstered pistol on their hip or a rifle slung on their shoulder. The strong proponents claim this is their right and argue it is nothing more than an extension of the CCW/CPL (carry concealed weapon / concealed pistol license) laws now in place in many states.

Even though I advocate the right of individuals to own and carry guns, a right guaranteed by the Second Article of the Bill of Rights, I have to wonder about other's basis for their argument. To be honest, I am prejudiced toward their argument. I am old enough to remember a time when many pick up trucks had gun racks mounted across the rear window, often seen with rifles or shotguns in place. Yet there is an aspect of the argument presented that I am not certain of. Rather than have a knee-jerk reaction to something that doesn't initially sit well with my way of thinking I want to consider the core issues prior to locking into a set position on the matter.

There is seemingly a contrast I have to work my way through. On one hand I have read about folks exercising their legal open-carry rights. They have caused no harm and responded appropriately when confronted by the police. CCW permit holders, of which I assume these people are many, are by-and-large law abiding, concerned citizens. They are not the ones you need to worry about. All that seems good, yet there is still an unknown in terms of something I was taught.

Several years ago I took a CCW class. The class was the first of a three-step process, of which I never got around to the remaining two, but licensure was not my objective. Rather, I wanted to know what the laws of my state do and do not allow. As I sat through the course very little was said about our rights. Maybe they were presumed. A lot, however, was said about our responsibilities.

If you legally carry a concealed weapon:
- You are responsible to be in control of your weapon at all times and to make sure it is concealed.
- You may not flash your weapon or show it off. Doing so is illegal.
- Rather than use your weapon, if you are able to withdraw from a situation without increasing risk to yourself or others that is what you are supposed to do. Thus, save macho for the movies.
- You only pull your weapon as a last resort, which means no viable option exists and the need for deadly force is present to protect yourself or others.

Even then, we were warned, even if you are 100% right in your actions, if you use your gun be prepared to spend the night in jail while the police sort everything out. An overriding theme that ran through the class was, as part of your CCW responsibility, you are to conduct yourself in such a manner that no one even knows when or if you are carrying a weapon.

Thus the conflict: The training that comes with CCW stresses the responsibility associated with the right; those who exercise open-carry are exercising their rights, but I don't know where they stand on accepting the responsibility.

I write this neither to defend nor reject one side or the other. Like I said earlier, I am still working through my thoughts on this matter. This is just a current issue that provides an opportunity to weigh our rights in balance to our responsibilities. These thoughts should not be construed as being for or against, nor meant to be in favor of one verses the other. Rights, responsibilities, and respect need to come as a package deal.

Now let's move away from the singular focus of the matter just presented and think on a broader scale. That will enable us to move toward the crux of this essay.

One point I hope to convey is that if we truly desire to have a peaceful, harmonious society, we have an obligation to exercise our rights respectfully and responsibly. Let me repeat that: If we truly desire to have a peaceful, harmonious society, we have an obligation to exercise our rights respectfully and responsibly. That applies to everybody, regardless of race, creed, color, or any of the other subgroup labels we like to use to segment our population.

Is that a great idea? Yup.

Do I think we will see a shift in societal attitudes to make that a reality? Nope.

Why? Because:
- We have a highly fractured society. We promote the fractures, and we tend to be suspicious of others.
- We are a self-centered society.
- There are many people who prosper nicely by working to ensure the afore mentioned stay that way. (Think of the exploits of certain social activists and the media's willingness to give them a prominent platform from which to pontificate; a willingness of politicians to distort truths at other people's expense all for the sake of taking a political, though not necessarily an honest, position; and a particular genre of the music and entertainment industry.)

We pay lip service to showing respect to others but societally we are not serious about it.

Socio-economic class status has nothing to do with this issue. It is about attitude. While I hope to see a change in direction of the way we behave, I will not be ignorantly blind to matters with which we currently have to contend. Let's pay attention to that.

Regarding the matter of our current condition, here are some points I believe we need to pay attention to:

* Do not be foolish or naive about what compels people to do the things they do.
* Do not be myopic in your assessments of what you see regarding other people's behavior.
* Those who embrace a belief in the goodness of man will find themselves both disappointed and vulnerable.

I do not advocate unwarranted aggression, but I do encourage people to be aware of their surroundings, both as it pertains to their physical presence, and as it pertains to the attitudes and mindsets of other people.

It is prudent to be gracious and courteous. It is equally prudent to be realistic and mindfully cognizant of human nature. Be observant, and maintain firm control of your emotions as you go about your activities. That statement contains an important implication: You should also be prepared to respond to situations accordingly. The admonition of President Teddy Roosevelt is still applicable today: "Walk softly and carry a big stick." Or as a friend of mine phrases it: "Be willing to take a punch before you throw a punch. But if you need to throw a punch make sure it accomplishes its intended purpose."

That last statement is not one that advocates aggression, it is simply an admonition to be mindful of ambient conditions. Be very mindful that there are mean, nasty, wicked people out there. Do not run from evil if it is your obligation to stand firm against it, yet it is prudent to avoid putting yourself in a vulnerable position if you have the ability to do so while not shortchanging others.

Many people express a concern that our society is becoming increasingly self-centered, and there is a plethora of evidence in support of that claim. The reasons for that, cause and effect, are plentiful. For an overview you may cite a degradation of societal norms as a contributing factor; the byproduct of institutionalized lies and half-truths spoken by prominent leaders may be another. Why trust anyone, or care about anyone, when you can't trust your leaders is the rationale behind that last statement. Perhaps it is just part of the life-cycle that every empire goes through, one step in a progression toward collapse. It is important that folks are cognizant of this but to also realize that the trend does not have to continue. Mindsets can change, and leaders can lead by example.

Very often we focus on an issue and run it through the mill of evaluation only to discover that which we are concerned about is a secondary issue, not a root cause. That which we so plainly see may be just a manifestation of a bigger problem. That may very-well hold true on this matter of rights and responsibilities.

I do believe there is opportunity for change, but that will have to come about by the actions of a younger generation than the one of which I am a part. My generation, the "Boomers", of which many of the goofballs now leading the free world are a part, focused way too much attention on rights, and not enough attention on responsibilities. Collectively you could call us the "I want it my way" generation. Perhaps subsequent groups will rightfully be labeled the "there is a better way" generation.

To understand what that "better way" needs to be you first need to define the root cause of what needs to change. Let's do that now.

I have come to believe that rights, respect, and responsibility are secondary considerations. How we choose to treat those "3 Rs" is based on how we treat "3 Gs": greed, grace, and gratitude.

* Greed is an ugly word, but it is a temptation we all face. It may be a mindset we more readily recognize in other people than we realize how it influences our actions. Greed is possessive, and it can be insidious. It does not always manifest itself in monetary or material ways.
* Grace is an attitude, a mindset, that constrains greed. Grace inclines our minds to think of others, not just ourselves.
* Gratitude does the legwork of grace. Gratitude is the catalyst that compels us to be dutiful in performing our responsibilities and in the subsequent actions we choose to undertake.

What do you think, is there sound reasoning in the above? We would be better off societally if we put greater emphasis on the 3 Gs. When you shift your focus from gratitude coupled with responsibility, to greed coupled to rights, your paradigm changes. Your mindset moves from being outwardly directed to inwardly directed. The shift advocates change without paying heed to what may be lost. Personally, I would like us to recover that which has been lost.

This essay has taken us all over the map, but that is not a bad thing. After all, one *Lesson After the Bell* is to gain a broad-picture perspective on issues so you can boil them down to root causes and considerations. You will then have valuable information with which you can make sound decisions. Maybe that is the crux of this essay.

There is probably a second essential issue, a second crux, as well. That is, societally choosing the standards by which we will abide. The good news is that you get to choose how you will live. The bad news is that so does everybody else. And to a certain extent, we all have to get along. So choose wisely. Be observant, be thoughtful, be wise, and give serious consideration to societally good choices. Recognize, too, the danger of being complacent, slothful, or foolish. Adopting a poise of being emotionally numb, emotionally lazy, or emotionally ignorant will work against you in the long-run. On certain matters diligence never gets to rest. You do not want to rely on other people's good judgement, because good judgement may not be there.

Prudent people always have a touch of suspicion that makes up their character. It is not there to antagonize or condescend. Rather, it is there to affirm the validity and truth of things they see, read, and hear. That is what I ask of you.

I have a friend, phenomenally well-educated and world-traveled, who often recites an African phrase. He speaks it in a dialect of the language he knows. I know when he uses the phrase, because I recognize the cadence of his words. Phonetically it sounds something like *"on enen shalla' en sala."* My friend tells me a rough interpretation of the phrase is: "In time we will see whom they are aiding."

So my admonition is to observe, consider, correlate, and pay attention to a big picture perspective. Note well how people's words align to their actions. In time you will truly see what others are advocating, and whom they are aiding.

Rights, respect, and responsibility need to be a package deal. They also need to be a two-way street. Metaphorically speaking, the package might look nicer, and the street might become a pleasant boulevard if we first commit to constraining greed, and consciously choose to abide in grace with gratitude. We need that for the betterment of society. Will you be one of those who choose to lead by example?

A Buck is a Buck, or So They Say

Ten dimes will get the job done. Twenty nickels will do the trick, too. I initially set out to determine how many combinations I could come up with to meet the objective. A couple of these and a hand full of those, so to speak. I bailed after only a short period of time, though. The combinations are more plentiful than I care to determine.

Who would have thunk it? After all, we only have four coins of the realm to contend with. Oh wait, there are some Kennedy half dollars floating around, and I completely neglected Sacaguea. So technically there are six coins of the realm. In reality though, you don't see much of Jack, and our Indian friend, though an important part of our nation's history she was,... Well, you just don't come across many of those. So it's OK to say four.

Let it suffice to say they all have value, even the lowliest of the bunch. As evidence of my belief in that statement, when I see one of those little guys lying unattended in a parking lot or on a sidewalk, I pick it up. By my line of reasoning if I do that a hundred-million times I will be a _____ (you figure it out). Better still, all that money will be mine tax-free. There's more too. Think of the workout: a hundred-million squats, a hundred-million reaches, a hundred-million lifts. Wow, I'll probably have the body of an Olympian. I can't wait, health and financial freedom!

Still, I think I'd rather have four of the big guys than a hundred of the smallest ones. For one thing its easier to keep track of the smaller group. With just a casual glance I know all are present and accounted for. Conversely, a casual glance at the large crowd leaves a bit of uncertainty. I can't discern the difference between seventy and a hundred unless I physically counted each one, and therein lies the problem. What if I'm anticipating some of those guys to be there, readily available, and they are nowhere to be found.

Perhaps I'm being too dogmatic on this issue. After all, I don't have segregated pockets, so whatever I have in my possession at any given time just travels as part of the crowd. I profess that I am not anti-copper, or whatever it is that those little fellas are made of, but I do have a silvery-metal inclination. I always want to have at least one of the big guys close by. I need them, I rely on them.

But in reality, with something close to five hundred words now written, this essay has nothing to do with pennies, nickels, dimes and quarters. The real issue is about relationships: close friends, good friends, friends, and others whom I know. Each group has different meaning, and intrinsically, different value.

A friend has a plaque that reads: "A good friend will come bail you out of jail. But a great friend will be sitting right beside you saying 'Gosh that was fun, lets do it again!'" I like that humor because it conveys an ideal, best of friends. But there is an implied condition that makes me quickly let go of the statement as I transition from concept to reality: What I really desire are friends who hold each other accountable, not those who hold each other hostage.

Those are the big guys - the quarters, the 25¢ pieces, two bits: friendships where there is a willingness to hold each other accountable. This can't be done with flippant regard, it is a right that is earned. Accountability is not used to tear down and damage. Rather, it is meant to build up. I am lucky. I have a dollar's worth of that type of friendship.

Now I need to think about the dime and nickel crowd. Though there are certainly distinctions in what creates the division between those categories - familiarity and opportunity for regular interaction, longevity of the relationship, commonality of interests, and other factors - it may be hard to define where one group stops and the other begins. Suffice it to say there are probably another couple bucks that can be added to the pot.

Then there is the next group. I find it marvelous and something to marvel at when I meet people who have a plethora of friends and acquaintances, more than can seemingly be counted. You may know someone in this category, or be one of those people yourself. My assumption is that they have both likable qualities and the inclination to want to know others. No matter where life takes them they keep adding new people to their address book; folks to be with for any occasion. Certainly this group is a part of my life too. The number isn't very big though. Jingle, but nothing near a dollar's worth.

When I do the math I consider myself rich, blessed. Quarters, dimes, nickels, and pennies; close friends, good friends, friends, and others whom I know. I am grateful for them all because each mean something of value to me. I can also lay claim to a Sacaguea and a couple Kennedys. I have wealth beyond measure.

I hope you get to walk around with a pocket full of change - pennies, nickels, dimes. Let me encourage you to make sure there are a couple quarters in there, too.

Now here's the rub. There is a challenge that comes with that hope. In order to have a friend worth so much, you have to be a friend who is worth a commensurate amount. Take the challenge. You may even find a Kennedy or Sacaguea. You don't come across many of those.

Facing the Facts and Comin' to Jesus

Here is a lesson worth learning: Make friends with people whom you want to emulate. People who possess character traits you admire; folks who have achieved a level of accomplishment, using whatever metric for evaluation you choose to employ, that you yourself want to achieve. I am told research supports the notion that you will gravitate toward and are most likely to become that which you hold close association with. If you want to become a high income earner associate with those who earn high incomes. If you want to develop your musical ability hang out with musicians. If you want to be an underachiever there are a myriad of groups you can be a part of. (I don't, by the way, advocate that last choice.) The long and short of this premise is that environmental factors do influence both how, and to what extent, people develop.

Ponder this for a moment and think how that may (should) influence your decisions regarding your involvements with others. Ponder also how this fact should compel you to take responsibility for your actions. They will be a determining factor in the selection process of people who may consider hanging out with you. That last sentence can be stated another way: Are you the type of person others want to be around and to emulate?

That notion of emulating those whom you admire may be why I have an affinity toward certain friendships. My friend Tammy, a teacher by training, is phenomenal when it comes to saying exactly the right words. She knows how to encourage and bring out the best in others. Her husband Mike, a friend whom I lived with in college, has a quick wit but not an ounce of bile. He makes me laugh like no one other. John is firm in his convictions and has the gift of oratory prowess. My interactions with each of these folks provide opportunities to see how they use attributes and abilities I hope to develop.

I find John particularly interesting because of how he puts his talents to work. He is a prolific reader, highly educated, and able to articulate thoughts clearly through verbal communication. While I share the first two attributes I struggle with the third. John's thoughts are well-organized, and when spoken there is an easy-to-follow stream of substantiating points. In discussion there is often the opportunity to pull in readily available ancillary information that support his premises. Very few, I suspect, are the people who take offense at his words even when they don't agree with him. He is kind, nonjudgemental, and genuine.

While I make every endeavor to provide firm foundations to my thoughts and beliefs, it frequently seems that my verbal presentations are rather clunky. It is almost a situation where my brain short-circuits and I have trouble speaking full sentences. That may be a bit of an exaggeration, but in a competitive environment I suspect any debate team would ask that I go join the other side. Therein lies the challenge for me: keep my brain from short-circuiting when provided the opportunity to articulate cogent thoughts.

This area of perceived weakness may be one reason I enjoy writing. There I have the opportunity to think clearly and analyze points both for clarity and precision. I'm not interested in being part of a debate, where the person with the best oratory skills or most chutzpah may prevail over a calmer, better-informed opponent. I am more concerned about articulating the truth, to and for the benefit of others. Thus, while I seek to develop in one area of communication I am grateful for another where I already have some proficiency.

I make comment of this both as a segue into another topic and as an opportunity to offer encouragement to others. Each of us has the ability to develop in whatever areas we want to be proficient. The timing, both commencement and duration, will be different from that of other people so we can't use their accomplishments as a tool to measure ours; there may be constraints that inhibit us from completing our goals, but every individual can move in the direction of their choosing. Even one step down the path of a long journey is still a first step taken, and there is value in that. If you are intent in your pursuit each successive step will be taken with greater confidence because each successive step moves you further down the path from where you began.

Here is an important fact to keep in mind. Remember this and use it as a source of inspiration and motivation when confronted with fatigue, weariness, and opposition: It is not where you begin that is important. What is important is where you are going. The focus isn't on the ending point, it is on the journey, your progression. Self-doubt and other forms of opposition will label you a failure; your counterstrike against those forces needs to be to affirm how far you have come, from where you were to where you are now.

Note what was not said earlier. I did not say each steps gets easier because that is not necessarily true. The further you progress, the more challenges you may face. That is simply a statement of reality. Therein lies an opportunity for motivation, too. You have set a course of development that requires self-motivation. That means you need to employ discipline and effort in order to enjoy accomplishment, and that is synonymous with the word work.

"Work" is a word to which people often attach negative connotations. I think it worth challenging that notion. Why degrade that which defines so much of what we are as individuals? Work is both that which enables us to meet the financial demands of today and provides greater opportunities for development and leisure in the future.

Hard work should be viewed by no one as being either undesirable or detrimental. Rather, it is a catalyst for accomplishment. In its physical application there are few things more satisfying than to be able to look back and think: "Look what I accomplished." For the corresponding mental application, the success is acknowledged by the opportunity to say: "Look what I now know." Both suggest the wise use of time and talents, which is commendable.

Work enables us to discover things about ourselves that we didn't before know. Exposure to certain situations may cause us to stretch and reach toward the vocation we choose as a career, something we might have once thought unattainable. In other situations work provides the experience to steer us away from that which we realize we are ill-suited.

It is important, however, to work smartly. Be sure that which you strive for, both through mental and physical endeavors, is well thought out, achievable, and worth the effort. Pursuits in matters that do not meet those criterion are fatiguing and a poor utilization of assets. Their net effect is that they move you backward, not forward.

Well, that took me in a direction I didn't originally plan to go. Now that I am completely off track from where I began let's jog back over to the purpose of this essay.

What got me started on that discourse on work is simply what I desire for others. I am all about people experiencing a fullness in life and having the opportunity to achieve all they are capable of achieving. Individually and collectively we have the capacity to accomplish more than what we often presume. As a society we do not give proper credence to the fact that, as part of the fully developed, governmentally stable, relatively disease-free Western world, our opportunities - health, sustenance, career & work, leisure & relaxation, accomplishments - are much greater than other parts of the world.

There are many people who do not appreciate that fact. The tendency of many is to degrade work (the need to apply oneself) as a hardship rather than celebrate and exercise the opportunities that are before them. I often wonder how (and why) those mindsets develops. Maybe they come about because we grew up hearing one burger joint telling us we can have things our way and another telling us we deserve a break. Perhaps we unwittingly buy into the proclamations of nationally known community organizers, activists, and politicians who tell us how bad things are, and greatly enrich themselves in the process. Maybe a contributing factor is the influence of unions that have negotiated the best pay and benefit packages for their members, yet readily fund the protests, through political contributions and other means, that destroy the mechanisms that provide for the unions' largesse.

This is crazy! I'm kinda thinking our paradigm is all screwed up. Just as it has taken many years for us to get to this point though, we can't make all the changes needed to get back on track overnight. If they come at all, they will take time.

I suppose I can take comfort in knowing we are not the only ones with strange notions. There are times where I see the attitudes of people from other countries expressed through their actions (sometimes inaction), or I hear someone of a different nationality talk about their perspectives and expectations, and I realize we are not alone in our folly. Even when I consider this though, I typically end up with the same three thoughts:

1. I expect more from us, the U.S., because we have so much.
2. I shouldn't expect perfection in a fallen world.
3. Maybe I can do some things to make a difference, and that is always an undertaking worth considering, but with certain issues it won't make much difference. That is a statement of fact and reality, not an excuse for not getting involved.

To the extent I am able, I do what I can. In the times I get to enjoy abundance I can be generous, both with time and talent, and with money. When my resources are stretched I do what I can, if I can. But I don't hold out hope that my efforts, either individually or in concert with a gazillion other people, will produce world peace, or end poverty, injustice, and cruelty. The reality is that global peace, with one exception, will never be upon us, and there will always be poverty, injustice, and cruelty. That is not a negative or defeatist attitude, it is just reality. The statement is accurate, so let's not hope for that which will not be. It is a poor utilization of assets.

There is a quote by George Santayana that fits well: "Only the dead have seen the end of war." I like Santayana's quote because it is a statement of truth. It is not negative; it is not defeatist or cynical. It is just a statement of fact and I like dealing with facts.

That does not exclude hope, though. Hope is something we should hold on to. This needs to be qualified though, the difference between the attainable and the unattainable.

There is rational hope: <u>hope that is well rooted; hope where there is a strong possibility that efforts properly employed will produce the results we desire</u>. This is not inconsistent with the statement I made a moment ago, because it is not a hope associated with delusional wishful thinking. A hope for the possible provides encouragement and the motivation to accomplish. There is a basis for this type of hope. It comes from acknowledging other things we know to be true, and building trust on those known truths. This hope stands in contrast to a hope for that not possible, wishful thinking. The latter is irrational and folly, and a poor utilization of resources.

Truth, well placed hope, and encouragement: Those seem like a good combination of facts and emotions that provide the catalysts for motivation and accomplishment. They provide a reason to be positive even when things are seemingly moving in a direction you prefer they not go. That is one of the sources of motivation for writing this book; something I "hope" folks will take from reading it: stay positive, with good reason; with truth and well-placed hope as a foundation, pursue whatever it is that you deem worthy of pursuing.

I have another reason for writing as well. It goes with the statement I made earlier regarding a fullness of life, that which I desire for everyone. My desire is subordinate, though, to individual people's actions.

My primary desire is that folks gain a perspective and clearly think through the process that will get them to understand, believe, and hold onto the ultimate value and purpose in life, a personal relationship with God through Jesus Christ. That is where you find a fullness of life, reason that fills the hollow places in your soul. This does not mean your life will be free from pain, doubt, hardship, and sorrow, but it can be one with well-placed hope that enables you to maintain a proper perspective.

It is not necessary that you first change, nor improve, nor become more knowledgeable. Start where you are now, and put a bit of thought into this simple concept: You have the opportunity to have a personal relationship with God. That opportunity comes through understanding that Jesus Christ creates the bridge between God and you. That is the key. By the way, it is God who built the bridge to man, not man who built the bridge to God.

That last point - the bridge-building one - is a critically important element that everyone should be aware of. Religion is man's effort at bridge-building. Every religion, including some doctrines that people assume to be Christian, boils down to man's efforts to become good enough to have a relationship with God. True unbridled Christianity starts with a simple recognition that man can never be good enough, and it is God who needs to initiate the connection. That connection has been established through Jesus Christ, and it can only exist through Jesus Christ. All other efforts are folly, and they do not succeed.

There it is. Those words just stated are my wish and my hope for you. People can encourage you to move in a certain direction, and I do, but the choice is yours. You have the opportunity to accept or reject. That is a freedom everyone gets to enjoy. The choice is always yours. It has to be that way, and I am fine with that.

A Meaningful Life

"So what, I am fine with that" is the comment I would offer. To which another involved in the conversation could reply: "Easy for you to say. You weren't the host, you didn't buy the dress, and you don't have to pay the dry cleaning bill." "Yeah, but you're missing the point" would be my response. "We had a great time, the wedding and reception were lots of fun, everyone got soaked by the deluge that occurred during the party following the reception, we all went away with fond memories, and the mud will come out of the hem of the bride's wedding dress (I think). Over time the memories grow and the negatives fade. Besides, who ever heard of a torrential downpour in Austin in September? That just made the evening all the more memorable."

Sometimes our outlook is simply a matter of perspective. Where we focus our attention dictates how we handle certain situations. Just like with rain during an outdoor wedding, you have to make the best of whatever occurs. With foreknowledge plans can be modified, but how often do we have that benefit? In reality it is not uncommon to have encounters like this. We have no option but to accommodate, shrug off the disappointment, and make the best of the situation.

There are other times though where a cavalier attitude is not sufficient. Times where serious situations cut us to the quick and afflict us with feelings of sadness, self-doubt, loneliness, and hopelessness. These are the emotions that have been bugging our bride of yesteryear lately. Things like this happen to everyone, but that provides little comfort when you are in the thick of the matter.

I encourage her to hang on. She is in a place I've heard referred to as the dark side of the desert. It is a place I have been, though perhaps with different pressures and conditions. It is not a particularly fun place to be - it's not fun at all - but you learn while you are there. The lessons enable you to move beyond the emotional pain. At some point you realize you have been blessed, and that which nearly destroyed you is no longer a part of you. Gone, never to return. This is a cathartic process, a stripping away of falsehoods in preparation of developing a depth of understanding not experienced before. It hurts, but the hurt does not last.

If I could wish for her I would wish for joy and peace. Joy is important, because it is not conditional on external circumstances. You can have joy even when things are going very poorly. Joy helps you maintain a proper perspective.

Peace is important too. It tells the voices screaming in your mind to be quiet. Peace says to the chaos: "You may have won a battle, but you will not win the war." With peace comes understanding and insight, understanding that the voices are lies, and insight as to who you are, a very important part of God's creation.

Wishing is just a sentiment, though. It has no power to change anything, so let's not dwell on that. Instead let's dwell on truth and reality, because therein lies the key to peace and joy. Therein lies a gift offered, waiting to be accepted.

The truth is in words I read as a young boy. They were painted on the side of a building near downtown Flint, Michigan, and I'd read them as I frequently passed by exercising the activities of my youth. They read:

> "For God so loved the world that he gave his only begotten son, that whoever believes in him should not perish but have everlasting life."

What this means is that we are important to God and we are purposefully created to have a personal relationship with him. The way God chose to do that is by having his son Jesus serve as our redeemer, a savior from our shortcomings, so we can enjoy the relationship God desires us to have. This is the gift offered, waiting to be accepted. It only requires that we ask Jesus, as Lord and Christ, our ultimate friend, into our lives.

I don't profess to understand the unknowns and the mysteries of God, and why he chooses to do things the way he does, but I don't need to either. By my line of reasoning, if you are the creator of the universe you can pretty-much do whatever you want, and since God is, he can. He doesn't have to ask my permission. I'm OK with this too, because I know man's comprehension and capacity for knowledge can't possible match God's. There is more to him and about him than I could ever realize. But I do know that he is the source of peace and joy. He stands against the evils that tell us lies.

Please don't dismiss this as religious gibberish because it is a simple truth that so many miss. We are a very important part of God's creation, the focal point of his creation. This is significant. God wants to have a personal relationship with each of us.

This notion is foreign to many. As a whole, we tend to reject it. That is too bad, because in so-doing those who so-choose set themselves up for colossal failure.

There is sometimes a lack of knowledge, so I encourage folks to investigate this and dig into it as if on a quest. Some let pride interfere. Pride manifests itself in many ways. Some get sidetracked and pick up silly notions about what God is or isn't, or think of him as a sugar-daddy. Avoid doing this. Some choose to worship science and man's self-sufficiency, or cosmic energy, or the environment, or Mother Earth, and in so doing worship the created instead of the Creator - dumb dumb dumb dumb dumb, and a wasted, useless effort.

What I hope for my friend (and you) is a fullness of life. It starts with pondering the verse listed above. Your pondering may lead to understanding, and understanding to believing. The three step process - ponder, understand, believe - is important, because that is what is necessary for developing a solid unwavering relationship that provides the foundation for peace and joy; a relationship built on knowledge, not emotion.

The words mentioned earlier are a passage from the Bible identified as John 3:16. There is another verse to consider as you start your quest. Proverbs 3:5-6 reads: "Trust in the Lord with all your heart, and lean not on your own understanding; in all your ways acknowledge him, and he will make your paths straight." (NIV) Ponder this also, and expectantly hold onto this notion. It will make more sense after you get a couple miles down the road and look back to reflect on what has occurred.

This assurance does not mean your path through life will suddenly become always pleasant and easy. It won't be that way and you will still have obstacles to work through. But it does affirm that you can prevail through whatever hardships you have to endure. Hardships, for all, are a part of life.

Some refer to this passage in Proverbs as proof that Christians are mindless automatons who believe whatever they are told. Ignore them, for they know not what they speak.

My encouragement is that you make today be the start of your quest to pursue a fullness of life and a satisfying life. Challenge me to see if what I wrote is true. God's offer stands open for anyone who chooses to accept it. The one condition is that you have to choose to accept it. It will not be forced upon you. The choice is yours.